CONSCIENCE AND CONFLICT:
British Artists and the Spanish Civil War

FIG. 1
HENRY MOORE (1898–1986)
Spanish Prisoner 1939
Uneditioned proof on English cartridge
36.5 x 30.5cm
The Henry Moore Foundation:
gift of the artist 1977

CONSCIENCE AND CONFLICT: British Artists and the Spanish Civil War

Simon Martin
Foreword by Paul Preston

PALLANT
HOUSE
GALLERY

Published to coincide with the exhibition
Conscience and Conflict:
British Artists and the Spanish Civil War
at Pallant House Gallery, Chichester
from 8 November 2014 to 15 February 2015

Touring to the Laing Art Gallery,
Newcastle-upon-Tyne
from 7 March to 7 June 2015

First published in 2014
by Pallant House Gallery

Pallant House Gallery
9 North Pallant, Chichester
West Sussex, PO19 1TJ
United Kingdom

www.pallant.org.uk

in association with

Lund Humphries
Wey Court East, Union Road
Farnham, Surrey, GU9 7PT
United Kingdom

and

Suite 3-1, 110 Cherry Street,
Burlington VT 05401-3818
USA

www.lundhumphries.com

Lund Humphries is part of Ashgate Publishing

Better Everyday

Headline sponsor of
Pallant House Gallery
2008 – 2014

Pallant House Gallery gratefully acknowledges
the Paul Mellon Centre for Studies in British Art
and De'Longhi who have supported the
cost of preparing this book. Our thanks also
go to supporters of the exhibition:

The Elephant Trust
The Henry Moore Foundation
The Idlewild Trust
The International Brigade Memorial Trust
The Mayor Gallery
The Conscience and Conflict Supporters' Circle

Edited by Miranda Harrison
Designed by David Wynn
Publishing Manager: Harriet Judd
Set in Foundry Sterling
Printed by L & S Printing, Worthing
Conscience and Conflict © Pallant House Gallery, 2014
Text © Simon Martin, 2014
Foreword © Paul Preston, 2014
Images: see Picture Credits

Hardback ISBN: 978-1-84822-175-8
Paperback ISBN: 978-0-70780-429-3
British Library Cataloguing in Publication Data:
A catalogue record for this book is available
from the British Library.

Library of Congress Control Number: 2014952422

Cover: John Armstrong, *The Empty Street*, 1938,
Tempera on panel, Private Collection
Fig. 1: Henry Moore, *Spanish Prisoner*, 1939,
Lithograph on paper, 36.5 x 30.5cm,
The Henry Moore Foundation

CONTENTS

FOREWORD
Paul Preston

FIG. 2
UNKNOWN
Help Spain 1937
Off-set lithograph on paper
75.5 x 49.2cm
Courtesy of the People's
History Museum

Albert Camus came near to accounting for the universal fascination with the Spanish Civil War when he wrote, 'It was in Spain that men learned that one can be right and still be beaten, that force can vanquish spirit, that there are times when courage is not its own reward. It is this, without doubt, which explains why so many men throughout the world regard the Spanish drama as a personal tragedy'. With moments that resonate with even those who know little or nothing of the Spanish conflict – the murder of Federico García Lorca, the arrival of the international volunteers in besieged Madrid, the bombing of Guernica, the flight of refugees across the Pyrenees – the civil war continues to generate passionate and often acrimonious debate 75 years after its end.

In all kinds of ways – geographical scale, the numbers of casualties, demographic consequences and technological horrors – the Spanish war has been dwarfed by later conflicts. Yet, over 30,000 books have been published on the conflict, and the work of the great chroniclers of the day, the newspaper correspondents and the photographers, is still cherished. At first this was partly the consequence of the fact that, for nearly 40 years, the dictatorship of the victorious General Franco churned out an interpretation of the war intended to justify his own regime. Both to humiliate the defeated, and to remind those implicated in the regime's networks of corruption and repression that only the Caudillo stood between them and the revenge of their victims, Franco's propagandists presented the war as a heroic, religious crusade against a barbaric Jewish-Bolshevik-Masonic conspiracy – portraying the vanquished as the dupes of Moscow and the blood-crazed perpetrators of sadistic atrocities. For the defeated Republicans and their foreign sympathisers the war was the struggle of an oppressed people for a decent way of life, against Spain's backward landed and industrial oligarchies and their Nazi and Fascist allies. That, in turn, provoked counter-efforts from both defeated Republicans and independent scholars the world over. However, Franco has been dead for nearly 40 years and the flood of books and documentary films shows little sign of abating.

In addition to the huge body of scholarly work the Spanish Civil War has a left a rich literary legacy in the books of Arturo Barea, George Orwell, Ernest Hemingway, André Malraux and many, many others. The articles of heroic war correspondents like Louis Delaprée, Geoffrey Cox, Herbert Matthews, Jay Allen, Louis Fischer and Henry Buckley retain their capacity to recall the passions of the war. The photographs of Robert Capa and Gerda Taro, of the Catalan Agustí Centelles, of the Frenchmen Jean Moral and Albert-Louis Deschamps, of José Juan Serrano, the man who recorded the exploits of Franco's African columns, and of so many others retain and indeed consolidate their iconic status. And yet, despite this wealth of material, there are two gaps – music and, perhaps more dramatically, the visual arts. Pallant House Gallery is now filling the gap as far as British visual artists are concerned. Coinciding with the 75th anniversary of the end of the conflict, this is the first major exhibition to showcase the way in which British artists reacted to the Spanish Civil War. The contents strikingly illustrate the commitment of

a generation of British visual artists largely on the Republican side, some going so far as to fight in the war themselves, others providing visual material for relief campaigns or raising awareness of the issues of the war through passionately political works of art. The much smaller number of artists who supported Franco are also represented.

In the light of the Second World War, Korea and Vietnam, and the wars of the Middle East and the Gulf, the Spanish Civil War may seem a forgettable squabble. After Hiroshima and Dresden the polemic provoked by the bombing of Guernica seems incomprehensible. Guernica may be kept alive by the power of Picasso's celebrated painting, but it is remembered above all because it was the first total destruction of an undefended civilian target by aerial bombardment. It is a reminder that the Spanish Civil War was a rehearsal for the bigger world war to come, opening the flood-gates to a new and horrific form of modern warfare that was universally dreaded. Sharing the collective fear of what defeat for the Spanish Republic might mean, more than 40,000 men and women, workers and

FIG. 3
ANON
An officer of the 43rd Division, at the welcoming of the 43rd Division at Gerona, Catalonia
c.1936–39
Black and white photograph
International Brigade Archive at the Marx Memorial Library
(Box 33A: 15/13A)

intellectuals went from all over the world to join the International Brigades. The Left saw clearly in 1936 what others chose to ignore: that when Madrid fell, Paris and London would be next. The volunteers believed that, if fascism could be defeated in Spain, it could be defeated in their own countries. Moreover, in the context of the harsh realities of capitalism during the great depression, they were also inspired by the revolutionary hopes of the Spanish experience. Before it was crushed by the necessities of the war effort, the collectivisation of industry and agriculture in Republican Spain seemed to be an exciting experiment. As Orwell commented, 'I recognized it immediately as a state of affairs worth fighting for'. In Spain the struggle against fascism could be seen as a first step to building a new egalitarian world out of the Depression. The anarchist leader Buenaventura Durruti summed this up when he declared: 'We are not afraid of ruins, we are going to inherit the earth. The bourgeoisie may blast and ruin their world before they leave the stage of history. But we carry a new world in our hearts.'

It is all too easy to see the Spanish Civil War in simple terms – as no more than communism against fascism or Christian civilisation against the barbaric hordes of Moscow. In fact, it was not one but many wars. It was a war of landless peasants against rich landowners, of anti-clericals against Catholics, of regional nationalists against military centralists, of industrial workers against factory owners. When Hitler, Mussolini and Stalin became involved, it became the first battle of the Second World War. Thus, the Spanish Civil War in its origins was a Spanish social war, and in its course and outcome it was an episode in a greater European Civil War that ended in 1945. The volunteers came to Spain with an instinctive understanding of both of these elements, an understanding shared by the majority of the writers, artists and photographers who responded to the war.

As Camus' words suggest, there is a strong case to be made for presenting the Spanish Civil War as the 'the last great cause'. As this exhibition reminds us, the Civil War inspired the greatest writers and artists of its day in a manner not repeated in any subsequent war. Moreover, it is impossible to exaggerate the sheer historical importance of the Spanish war. Beyond its climactic impact on Spain itself, the war was very much the nodal point of the 1930s. Baldwin and Blum, Hitler and Mussolini, Stalin and Trotsky all had substantial parts in the Spanish drama. The Rome-Berlin Axis was clinched in Spain at the same time as the inadequacies of appeasement were ruthlessly exposed. Franco believed, rightly, that he had done Hitler an enormous service in defeating the Republic because of the way in which he had exposed the weakness of appeasement and specifically altered the balance of power against the Western allies, both internationally and also in terms of internal French politics. A Republican victory might have stiffened French resistance, it might have avoided the Hitler-Stalin pact, it may have severely dented Mussolini's confidence, and it may possibly even have avoided the Second World War altogether. However, that is mere speculation. What is certain is that the artists of the day perceived, as the politicians did not, the implications of what was happening in Spain.

LA LUCHA DEL PUEBLO ESPAÑOL POR SU LIBERTAD

INTRODUCTION:
Conscience and Conflict

FIG. 5
R.B. KITAJ (1932–2007)
'La Lucha del Pueblo
Español Por su Libertad'
from the series
In Our Time: Covers for a
Small Library After the Life
for the Most Part
1969–70
Screenprint on paper
77 × 57.5 cm
Pallant House Gallery:
Wilson Gift through
The Art Fund (2006)

The Spanish Civil War (July 1936 – April 1939) was arguably one of the most politically and socially significant conflicts of the twentieth-century. Described by Ernest Hemingway as 'the dress rehearsal for the inevitable European war',[1] the Civil War was far more than an internal binary conflict between the left-wing, democratically elected Spanish Republicans and the right-wing Nationalist insurgents led by General Francisco Franco – it was a battle-ground for various opposing ideologies in the 1930s. A huge amount has been written about the complex and contested history of the Spanish Civil War, and it is often commented that despite the Nationalist victory in 1939 and the many partisan accounts that were published by the authoritarian dictatorship of General Franco until 1975, the history of the conflict has largely been written by the losers, defying the adage that history is always written by the winners. It is still the subject of great fascination today, and in Spain it is to some extent an open wound that has never entirely healed.

Despite the many gruesome accounts of brutality – carried out by both sides – the Spanish Civil War has been subject to much mythmaking and romanticism. Perhaps this is in part due to the fact that it has existed in the popular imagination as a 'literary' conflict, recorded and brought to life by active participants in the field, as in *Homage to Catalonia* by George Orwell (who fought with the Trotskyite POUM – Workers' Party of Marxist Unification) and *For Whom the Bell Tolls* by Ernest Hemingway. Stephen Spender memorably described it as the 'poets' war'[2] reflecting the significant number of poets and writers who went from Britain and Ireland to volunteer in various capacities in Spain, including W.H. Auden, David Gascoyne, John Cornford, Valentine Ackland, Ewart Milne, Sylvia Townsend Warner, Roger Roughton, Julian Bell and Spender himself, not to mention the many others who wrote poetry in response to the conflict without being directly involved in the field. In 1937 Nancy Cunard's survey 'Authors Take Sides on the Spanish War' was published by *Left Review*, presenting the responses of a cross-section of writers and poets to the question: *'Are you for, or against, the legal Government and the people*

of Republican Spain? Are you for, or against, Franco and Fascism?' The result was a fascinating overview of literary opinions: 16 neutral including T.S. Eliot and Vita Sackville-West; 5 replies 'Against the Government' including Edmund Blunden and Evelyn Waugh; and 127 in support of the Government including Samuel Beckett (who simply declared '¡UPTHEREPUBLIC!'), Cyril Connolly, Cecil Day Lewis, Havelock Ellis, Ford Maddox Ford, Aldous Huxley, John Lehmann, Rose Macaulay, V.S. Pritchett and Leonard Woolf, amongst many others. As Louis MacNeice was to observe in his *Autumn Journal,* in Spain 'our blunt ideals would find their whetstone...'[3] In contrast to the writers and poets, the deep engagement of British artists in the Spanish Civil War conflict has not received the same level of attention; there are various possible reasons for this. There are far fewer literary accounts of artists' experiences; many of the most directly responsive artworks – banners, billboards, and posters – were by their very nature ephemeral (such politically engaged works have often

been treated as exceptions to an artist's wider *oeuvre*); and the Civil War was overshadowed by the all-consuming Second World War, even though Spain undoubtedly informed many artists' images of the suffering and devastation of war. Surprisingly, there are virtually no books written specifically about British art and the Spanish Civil War, and even the admirable exhibition *The Spanish Civil War: Dreams and Nightmares* at the Imperial War Museum in 2001 only featured a handful of works by British artists.[4] The prevailing view has been that there was nothing created in Britain to compare with the intensity and power of Picasso's *Guernica* (fig.7), painted in 1937 in response to the bombing of the eponymous town. This is undoubtedly true, but then very few works by any artist of the twentieth-century can compare with Picasso's iconic masterpiece, which has come to represent the suffering of humanity more widely in modern warfare. Picasso's *Guernica* is, however, an integral part of the story of Britain and the Spanish Civil War. Brought to London and Manchester

FIG. 6
Photograph of girl in the P.O.U.M. militia (Workers' Party of Marxist Unification) Militia (n.d.)
Black and white photograph
12 x 16.5cm
The International Brigade Archive, Marx Memorial Library, London
(Box A-3: F/14)

FIG. 7

Interior of the Spanish Republican Pavilion at the Paris World Fair with Pablo Picasso's *Guernica*, 1937

in 1938–9 by the Surrealist artist Roland Penrose and others, it was seen by thousands of working-class men and women, as well as many artists on whom it had a profound impact. In 1937 Myfanwy Evans, in her essay *The Painter's Object,* was to observe a difference in the way that non-Spanish artists engaged aesthetically with the Civil War:

> Moore is not a Spaniard, nor is Nash, nor Hélion, nor Léger, nor any of the others in this book, and their only way of dealing with the immediate problems of Spain is not to *act* as well as paint or carve, not to become for the moment Spaniards and try and express the revolution (and resolve it) as if it were their own … not even to try to feel what they would feel *if* all this were happening in their own country – that is, a kind of perverted spiritual whoring – but to treat the war in Spain as part of the existing world, part of the world to which they have to find an answer in their own way, the world which as it was during the great war Picasso expressed through the wineglass and the guitar.

But whilst this was true to some extent, many artists including Moore did become increasingly and more directly engaged during the period 1936 to 1939. Numerous British artists had visited or lived in Spain during the 1920s and early 1930s, attracted by the country's sun-baked landscapes, the inexpensive artist colonies, the accessible exoticism of bullfights and flamenco dancers, the artistic treasures in the Prado and, in the case of artists such as Leon Underwood and Henry Moore, the pre-modernism of the Altamira Caves and other sites. Artists including Muirhead Bone, William Russell-Flint, Augustus John, William Nicholson, Wyndham Lewis, Tristram Hillier, David Bomberg and Edward Burra were all in the country in the years before the Civil War, as were many others who exhibited numerous Spanish scenes in venues such as the Royal Academy. Several of these, including Bomberg and Burra, had to leave due to the violence before the outbreak of the Civil War; George Bergen encountered 'corpses in the streets' of Barcelona before his departure in the summer of 1936.[6]

Of those who engaged with the fate of
Spain after July 1936 most were doing so, not
because of a developed understanding of the
country and its culture, but because they saw it
in simple terms as a matter of freedom against
tyranny and fascism. Speaking of the need to be
political, the literary critic Cyril Connolly observed
that,'Today the forces of life and progress are
raging on one side, those of reaction and death
on the other. We are having to choose between
democracy and fascism, and fascism is the enemy
of art. It is not a question of relative freedom;
there are no artists in Fascist countries'.[7]

The question of British political involvement
in the Spanish Civil War was to be the subject of
heated debate in parliament and the media, against
a background of widespread unemployment due to
the Great Depression and concerns over the rise
of fascism in Europe, the spread of communism
from the Soviet Union, and safeguarding the
interests of the British Empire. Britain signed a Non-
Intervention Agreement, together with 24 other
nations, in August 1936. Due to a Franco-British

HOLIDAY SPECIAL
TOURISTS ONLY

TO TIMBUKTOO VIA LISBON

HARMLESS HIKING CLUB ONLY

FOR PRIVATE USE ONLY

BANANAS ONLY PORTUGAL

THE NON-INTERVENTION COMMITTEE DECIDE TO WAIT UNTIL THE WAR ENDS BEFORE TAKING A FIRM STAND.

LOW

OLD LOW'S ALMANACK.   PROPHECIES FOR 1937

FIG. 10
DAVID LOW (1891–1963)
Cartoon from the
Evening Standard
23 December 1936

arms embargo the Spanish Republic could only purchase arms from the Soviet Union, yet large amounts of weapons, supplies and troops were provided to General Franco and his Nationalist rebels by Nazi Germany and fascist Italy, escalating the situation from a civil war to a conflict with an international dimension.[8] Many, including the British Surrealist Group, called for 'Arms for Spain', asserting that non-intervention was essentially tacit support for the Nationalists and their allies. The cause of Republican Spain attracted widespread support as it provided an opportunity for people and organisations from a wide political spectrum to show solidarity against fascism.

In Britain views ranged from support for Oswald Mosley and his British Union of Fascists (known as the 'Blackshirts') on the far right, to those who sought appeasement, non-intervention and a pacifist solution, and the Communist Party members who demanded direct intervention to avoid a much wider European war. According to art historian Anthony Blunt, writing in the 1960s (before his exposure as a Soviet agent),

it is hard for anyone who was not grown-up at the time to realise the importance of the Spanish Civil War to intellectuals in Western Europe. There were many, particularly in England, but also to a lesser degree in France, who could still delude themselves into believing that Communism was a matter which primarily concerned Russia, and that Fascism was an affair for Central Europe. The Spanish war raised the issue of Fascism versus Democracy to a different plane, it brought it to Western Europe, and it gave it the form of an armed conflict instead of the persecution of a minority. Even for the most ivory tower intellectual it meant that the time for not taking sides was past; the conflict was too near and involved too many of one's personal friends.[9]

Of the more than 40,000 men and women who went from 53 countries to join the International Brigades to fight for the Republican cause, around 2,500 were from Britain. Recruited by the Communist Party of Great Britain these volunteers

THERE IS NO PEACE

H. RAYNER

FIG. 11
HENRY RAYNER (1902–57)
There is No Peace 1936
Etching on paper,
signed in pencil
10.7 x 16.5 cm
Ron Heisler Collection

were largely from the working classes, but also included many intellectuals, and even upper-class fellow travellers such as Esmond Romilly, nephew of Winston Churchill. Their role was summed up by Dolores Ibárruri, communist MP from Asturias popularly known as '*La Pasionaria*' (passion-flower), in her emotional address at the farewell parade for the International Brigades in Barcelona at the end of October 1938:

> Comrades of the International Brigades! Political reasons, reasons of state, the good of that same cause for which you offered your blood with limitless generosity, send some of you back to your countries and some to forced exile. You can go with pride. You are history. You are legend. You are the heroic example of the solidarity and the universality of democracy … We will not forget you; and, when the olive tree of peace puts forth its leaves, entwined with the laurels of the Spanish Republic's victory, come back!

British artists who fought in Spain included Felicia Browne, who joined a communist militia in August 1936 and was the first British individual killed in the conflict (in advance of the International Brigades being formed); Clive Branson, who created memorable images of Spanish prison camps as well as poetry; the landscape painter Wogan Phillips who volunteered as an ambulance driver; the cartoonist W.D. Rowney ('Maro') who was killed in 1937; and Jason Gurney, whose career as a sculptor was ended after he was shot through the hand.[10] Others attempted to join the International Brigades, such as 15 year-old Michael Ayrton who was recalled by his mother the Labour politician Barbara Ayrton Gould, and the illustrator Paul Hogarth who joined aged 17 but was repatriated. Numerous others went out to Spain, including the Surrealists S.W. Hayter, John Banting and Roland Penrose, while others such as Henry Moore and Jacob Epstein were prevented from doing so by the British government. The question of direct action versus artistic creation was much discussed, particularly by the left-wing communist Artists

FIG. 12
Dolores Ibárruri (1895–1989)
– known as 'La Pasionaria' –
speaking at a rally in the 1930s
The International Brigade
Archive at the Marx
Memorial Library

FIG. 13
RB KITAJ (1932–2007)
La Pasionaria c.1965
Oil on canvas
31 x 33.2 cm
Private Collection

International Association (AIA), which had over 600 members by 1936 and organised many of the exhibitions, events, poster campaigns and fundraising activities for Spain. Artistic support for Republican Spain crossed every form of artistic style in an art world that was composed of numerous competing and overlapping groups. As Myfanwy Evans was to observe of these contradictory times:

> we have got into the middle of not one but a thousand battles. Left, right, black, red (and white too, for the fools who won't take part and so constitute a battle line all on their own), Hampstead, Bloomsbury, surrealist, abstract, social realist, Spain, Germany, Heaven, Hell, Paradise, Chaos, light, dark, round, square. 'Let me alone – you must be a member – have you got a ticket – have you given a picture – have seen *The Worker* – do you realise – can you imagine – don't you see you're bound to be implicated – it's a matter of principle. Have you signed the petition – haven't you a picture more in keeping with our aims – *intellectual freedom,* FREEDOM *FREEDOM* – we must be allowed, we can't be bound – you can't, you must fight – you *must*.[11]

Evans' phrase '*haven't you a picture more in keeping with our aims*' highlights the conundrum faced by many artists that were working in non-figurative styles, particularly the Surrealists and Abstractionists. Writing to Portia Holman, Secretary of the Spanish Medical Aid Committee, Bloomsbury artist Vanessa Bell whose son Julian had died in Spain in July 1937 confessed that, 'it was rather difficult to think of something that was non-religious, had some connection with Spain and wasn't too gloomy for Christmas. I don't know if I've succeeded'.[12] The subject of many of the paintings donated to exhibitions in support of Spanish relief had nothing to do with the conflict – for example, the *White Reliefs* exhibited by Ben Nicholson at AIA exhibitions in support of Spain could not be read as having any political content, except perhaps through their aesthetic freedom and affinity to the so-called 'Degenerate art' recently outlawed in Nazi Germany. In *Letter to Lord Byron* (1937)

W.H. Auden expressed the idea that artists had lost contact with their audiences as individualistic creators without any responsibility to their audiences:

> A new class of creative artist set up
> On whom the pressure of demand was let up
> He sang and painted and drew dividends
> But lost responsibilities and friends

According to Auden, those 'who feel most like a sewer belong to Painting not to Literature':

> As long as art remains a parasite,
> On any class of persons it's alright;
> The other thing it must be is attendant,
> The only thing it mustn't, independent.

Even abstract artists such as Barbara Hepworth and Alastair Morton created atypical works that directly reference Spain, such as Hepworth's *Project: Monument to the Spanish Civil War* (fig. 14) and Morton's *Spanish Civil War* (fig. 48), whilst John Piper designed an abstract rug that was made by miner's wives to be auctioned.[13] When around 90 artists took to painting billboard hoardings for Spain in February 1939, or creating banners and floats for the May Day processions, they were taking their work into the world to engage directly with non-elite audiences. Yet the question of relevance and the ability of modernist art to convey an understandable message was to be much discussed by the members of the AIA, leading to various disagreements between the Surrealists and Realists. Beyond the immediacy of posters for Spanish aid created by the likes of E. McKnight Kauffer, Frank Brangwyn and Felicity Ashbee, much has been written about whether modernist art can serve as propaganda, but it would seem that it was ultimately about the way in which an image is used, and the context in which it used. Myfanwy Evans asked the rhetorical question for artists: 'Does he get involved in squalor and bloodshed as a politician or an organiser or an adventurer in order to evade the immediate problems of his art, does he allow propaganding, fighting, slumming (perfecting even) to get so important that painting or sculpture, or whatever he does, becomes a sideline – real escapism if you like?[14]

FIG. 14
BARBARA HEPWORTH
(1903–75)
Project: Monument to the Spanish Civil War
1938–39
Plan wood, maquette
Dimensions unknown
Destroyed in World War II

This exhibition and publication seek to reconsider the role of British artists in the Spanish Civil War – and to consider how and why the conflict touched individuals' consciences and made them want to act in some way. It brings together material from a range of sources, and in a variety of media, to demonstrate the extent to which artists engaged with a civil war in another country. It is often stated that British art in the first-half of the twentieth-century was somehow insular, or operating in a vacuum, but organisations such as the AIA, the activities of the Surrealist Group, and the deep commitment to action on behalf of the Spanish Republic show that the truth is far more complex. It is also important to remember that artistic support was by no means entirely for the Republicans. Individuals such as Sir Francis Rose, William Russell-Flint and Wyndham Lewis were to varying degrees pro-Franco (although Lewis' position was complicated and inconsistent – later in the war he gave Julian Trevelyan a painting to be sold in support the Republicans).

The Spanish Civil War has been described as 'the last great cause', and as Stanley Weintraub has stated: 'Never since has a cause captured the moral and physical influence of so many makers and molders [sic] of the language, or created such relentless pressure upon so many members of the intellectual communities in the English-speaking world to take side, to make a stand'.[15] It perhaps for these reasons that it continued to inspire artists in the years after the war ended. R.B. Kitaj created several paintings and prints in the 1960s dealing with themes from the Spanish Civil War, including his painting *La Pasionaria* (fig. 13) depicting Dolores Ibárruri giving an impassioned speech; the enigmatic *Junta* (fig. 15), featuring an imaginary revolutionary junta including a figure based on the anarcho-syndicalist militant Buenaventura Durruti; and two of his series of book jackets *In Our Time: Covers for a Small Library After the Life for the Most Part* (1969–70): *La Lucha del Pueblo Español* (fig. 5) and *Kampflieder: Battle Songs: Canzoni di Guerra*, a facsimile of the cover of *Canciones de Guerra de la Brigades Internacionales*. Others, such as the abstract artists Terry Frost and Sean Scully, have been inspired by the poetry of the Spanish poet and dramatist Federico García Lorca who was killed by pro-Franco forces on 19 August 1936. In the 1980s Frost created a portfolio of prints entitled *Eleven Poems by Federico García Lorca* responding to the visceral imagery of Lorca's poetry (fig. 18). More recently contemporary artist Goshka Macuga has created a charged installation in the Whitechapel Art Gallery to revisit the extraordinary visit of Picasso's *Guernica* to the same gallery in 1939 (fig. 17).

Included in the present exhibition are works by Spanish artists such as Picasso and Miró that were exhibited in the UK in the 1930s and collected by British artists. A new textile version of Picasso's *Guernica* will be presented, made at collaborative sewing workshops involving volunteers from Amnesty International, Brighton

FIG. 15
R.B. KITAJ (1932–2007)
Junta 1962
Oil and collage on canvas
91 x 213 cm
Private Collection

FIG. 16
R.B. KITAJ (1932–2007)
'What is a Comparison'
(1964) from the series
*Mahler Becomes Politics,
Beisbol 1964–67*
colour screenprint and
photo-screenprint on paper
78.5 x 58 cm
Pallant House Gallery:
Wilson Gift through
The Art Fund (2006)

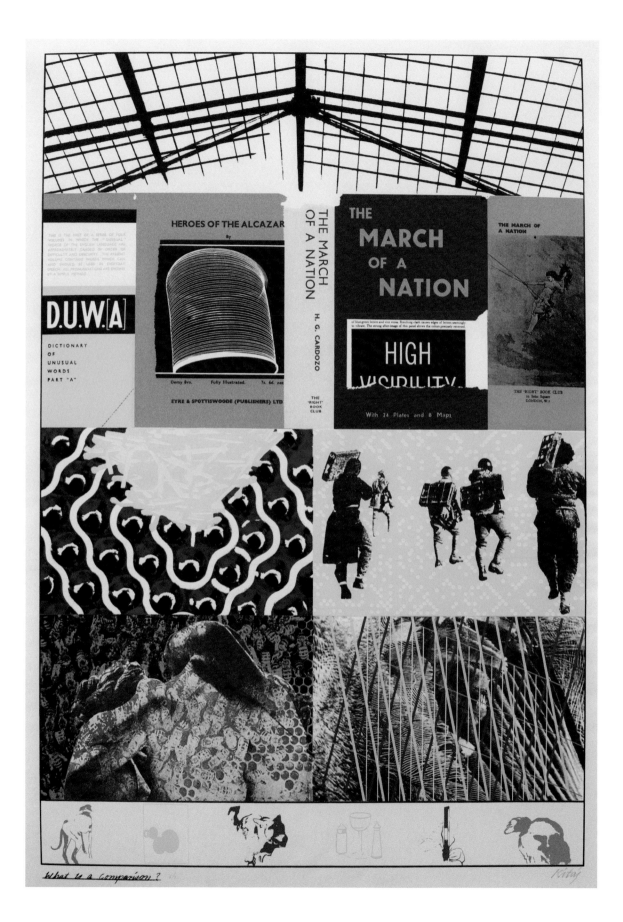

Anti-Fascists, Gatwick Detainee Visitors, the Migrant English Project, the Palestine Solidarity Campaign, the University of Brighton and the Women's International League for Peace and Freedom – making clear the ongoing relevance of the imagery and themes in the exhibition to contemporary events in Syria, Iraq and the Ukraine, and other countries.

Organisations such as the International Brigade Memorial Trust and the Marx Memorial Library in particular have been enormously helpful with this exhibition, but it could not have been put together without information, advice and support from many individuals and organisations (see Acknowledgements) – or the generosity of lenders who have allowed us to show their works at Pallant House Gallery and the Laing Art Gallery, and the hard work of our staff. The exhibition has been generously supported by the Henry Moore Foundation, the Elephant Trust, the IBMT, the Mayor Gallery, the Paul Mellon Centre for Studies in British Art, and the *Conscience and Conflict* exhibition Supporters Circle, to whom we are immensely grateful. It is surprising that an exhibition on this theme has not been mounted before, but it would not have happened if the Surrealist collector Dr Jeffrey Sherwin had not come to me with the original suggestion for an exhibition about the Spanish Civil War. I am indebted to him for his passion and commitment. It has been a great privilege to bring together such extraordinary material, reminding of the importance of art and artists to society, and the fact that they can and do make a difference.

This exhibition marks the 75th anniversary of the end of the Spanish Civil War in 1939. It is a testament to the creativity and intention of the artists that the works within it remain moving and arresting so many years after the conflict has ended; they transcend being journalistic or transitory statements to being expressions of something deeper about humanity. The story of those whose conscience led them to create these artworks, or to volunteer to fight, to serve in medical aid, or to assist with the Spanish refugees in this country or in France, is inspirational.

FIG. 17
GOSHKA MACUGA
(b. 1967)
The Nature of the Beast
2009
Mixed media installation,
Whitechapel Art Gallery

FIG. 18
TERRY FROST (1915–2003)
'Lament for Ignacio
Sánches Mejias' from
*Eleven Poems by
Federico García Lorca* 1989
Etching on paper
55.7 x 37.8 cm
Austin/Desmond Fine Art

1. Ernest Hemingway, in Carlos Baker (ed.), *Ernest Hemingway: Selected Letters 1917–1961* (New York: Scribner, 1981), p.348.
2. Stephen Spender in Richard Crossman (ed.), *The God that Failed* (New York: Harper and Brothers, 1950).
3. Louis MacNeice, *Autumn Journal* (London: Faber & Faber, 1939).
4. A notable exception is Professor Tom Buchanan's essay 'Mobilising Art: British artists and the Spanish Civil War' in Buchanan 2007, to which this exhibition is indebted.
5. Evans 1937.
6. Vanessa Bell to Julian Bell, 5 September 1936, Tate Gallery, Julian Bell papers, TGA 9311. Quoted in Buchanan, *ibid.*, p.87.
7. Cyril Connolly, *Enemies of Promise* (London: Routledge & Kegan Paul, 1938), p.2.
8. Conquest, Robert, *Stalin: Breaker of Nations* (London: Viking, 1991), p.219. Stalin apparently sent 648 aircraft and 407 tanks, and 3,000 Soviet 'volunteers'
9. Anthony Blunt, *Guernica* (Oxford: Oxford University Press, 1969), p.8.
10. See Jason Gurney, *Crusade in Spain* (London: Faber & Faber, 1974), p.174.
11. Evans, *ibid.*, p.5.
12. Letter from Vanessa Bell to Portia Holman, November 1938, Tate Gallery Archives, TGA 8511.9.
13. See Morris 1983, p.33.
14. Evans, *ibid.*, p.6.
15. Weintraub, Stanley, *The Last Great Cause: Writers and the Spanish Civil War* (London: W.H. Allen, 1968), p.2.

1 CULTURE WARS: British Engagement with the Plight of Spain's Artistic Heritage

During the opening months of the Spanish Civil War, there was much consternation in Britain at reports of the destruction and seizure of churches and other religious buildings, private homes, and artistic treasures in anti-clerical actions by revolutionary militias. In October 1936 a symptomatic photograph appeared in the British press in which manuscripts and books from the Bishop's palace at Vic in Catalonia were piled up in the town square. Around 150 churches were completely destroyed and nearly 5,000 were damaged in some way. In September 1936 Nationalists issued the first Burgos *Official Report*[1] and a subsequent *Joint Letter* in which they declared that 'the revolution was "barbarous", inasmuch as it destroyed the civilising work of centuries'.[2] As the historian Hugo García has asserted, for most of the Civil War the Nationalists:

> insisted that the 'Reds' had destroyed *all* the religious buildings in their half of Spain, which naturally gave the authorities in Salamanca and Burgos an excuse not to provide any numbers on the extent of the destruction

... In March 1939 *Spain* magazine raised the number of churches and related buildings that had been burnt out to 25,000, a figure possibly greater that the entire number of religious buildings in Spain at that time.[3]

Soon after the start of the war the Republican government had established the *Junta de Incautación y Protección del Tesoro Artistico* (Council for the Confiscation and Protection of Artistic Treasures) – headed by the painter Don Timoteo Pérez Rubio – in order to prevent cultural vandalism and emphasise the importance of Spain's heritage. Conscious of the need to counter the Nationalist's claims Jaume Miravitlles,[4] who headed the Generalitat's Propaganda Commissariat, invited Christian Zervos, editor of the French art journal *Cahiers d'Art*, to Barcelona to collect material for a new book on Catalan art. The book was to be 'based on newly discovered works which had been discovered shortly after the outbreak of the War, in the houses of exiled, executed Fascists, now requisitioned by the Government and also in churches, cathedrals, etc.'[5] Zervos was joined by the British Surrealist artist Roland Penrose, and from October to December 1936 they toured heritage sites in towns and cities in Catalonia – including Barcelona, Vic, Gerona, Lérida, Tarragona and Valencia – with a group that included the Surrealist poet David Gascoyne, a painter called Fernandez, the Catalan art promoter Joan Prats, and the architect and art historian Josep Mariá Gudiol. The outcome of Penrose and Zervos' trip was the book *Catalan Art from the Ninth to the Fifteenth Centuries,* published in 1937. Illustrated with copious black and white photographs of artworks, it featured texts on Romanesque and Gothic architecture, sculpture and painting by Fernna Soldevila and Gudiol, with a preface co-penned by Zervos and Penrose on 'Art and the Present Crisis in Catalonia'. The latter text opened with the lines, 'in a country shaken by military revolt, civil war and revolution the question as to who are the natural guardians of the cultural inheritance confronts us in the light of natural events'.[6] Their preface documented the efforts of the Republicans to protect Catalan art of the Romanesque and Gothic periods, and almost dismissively noted that the church burnings had been of 'minor examples of the baroque period, whose gilded shame excited particularly the vengeance of the people'.[7] They reported that less than two per cent of Catalonia's artistic heritage had been lost and as Penrose later recalled, 'we were able to state that in spite of some revolutionary acts of violence, chiefly in Barcelona, the monuments had been revered and protected, in some cases more efficiently by the Republican regime than by the Church, which had often either neglected or sold its treasures'.[8]

During the Nationalist bombing campaign against Madrid in November 1936 Pérez Rubio made plans to remove more than 500 of the greatest artistic treasures of the Prado and other museums to the Republican capital of Valencia,

and subsequently to the Palace of the League of Nations in Geneva.[9] The bombing of prominent monuments in Madrid such as the Prado, Biblioteca Nacional and the Palacio de Liria by Nationalist aircraft was, in the words of the historian Álvarez Lopera, a 'real gift' for the Republican propaganda services. Images of damage to the Prado were distributed around Europe within 48 hours, and subsequently featured in documentary films such as Ivor Montagu's *Defence of Madrid*.[10] In 1937 the Republicans produced a series of pamphlets called *Fascism Destroys Spain's Art Treasures* in Spanish, English and French, in which their own protective activities were contrasted with 'fascist barbarism'. On 20 July a letter from Sir Frederic Kenyon, former director of the British Museum (written at the encouragement of his friend, Franco's representative in London the Duke of Alba), was published in *The Times*, calling on the Republican government to explain its measures to protect Spain's artistic heritage. The move was to backfire on the Duke of Alba, for the *Daily Telegraph* published a letter from the Pro-Republican Viscount Hastings (a practicing artist who had trained with Diego Rivera in Mexico; see fig. 9) in which he described the evacuation of artworks from the Prado and his personal inspection of the vaults in Valencia where Goyas, Titians and El Grecos were being stored.[11] Kenyon's letter resulted in an invitation from Pablo

FIG. 21
IGNACIO ZULOAGA
(1870–1945)
Seige of the Alcázar 1938
Oil on canvas
145 × 173 cm
Former collection of
Ramón Suárez Zuloaga,
stolen and missing

de Azcárate, the Spanish Republic's ambassador to London, for Kenyon to visit Republican Spain, which he did with James G. Mann, Keeper of the Wallace Collection, in August 1937. Returning convinced of the Republic's good work they published articles for *The Times* and *The Daily Telegraph*, praising measures to protect Spain's artistic treasures, and reporting on the safety of the Prado's treasures in Valencia.[12] Their reports subsequently featured in the pamphlet *Art Treasures of Spain* published by the Republican Embassy in London.

Although the Nationalists' claims about the pillaging and trafficking of works of art taking place in the Republican territories may have had some basis in fact, any credibility was undermined by their frequently spurious claims. In one instance the accusation that the Republican government had stolen and sold El Greco's *Burial of Count Orgaz* (1586–8) from the Church of St Thomas in Toledo had to be refuted in *The Times* on 23 February 1937 by the Spanish ambassador Azcárate. Eventually, in August of that year, the Nationalists acknowledged that the painting had been in their hands since

their highly symbolic Nationalist victory over the Popular Front militias on 27 September 1936.

To the Nationalists the Alcázar of Toledo signified the strength and dominance of Spain, as it had been the residence of the Spanish monarchs after the re-conquest of Toledo from the Moors (although, ironically, Franco's victory in Toledo was due to the presence of the Army of Africa, which included Moorish troops). The siege of the Alcázar was the subject of a major painting, referencing El Greco's paintings of the city by the Nationalist supporter Ignacio Zuloaga (fig. 21). The painting was to be the centrepiece of an exhibition of 45 Zuloaga works at the New Burlington Galleries in London in December 1938. Although several scholars have suggested that the exhibition was shown concurrently with Picasso's *Guernica*, in fact the exhibitions took place several weeks apart.[13] Even so, the alluring comparison between the former friends and compatriots – the abstraction of *Guernica* versus Zuloaga's realistic paintings of 'Old Spain' – serves to highlight the starkly contrasting ideological positions between the artistic avant-garde and the Republican cause, and the Nationalists with more conservative artistic styles.

The idea for the Zuloaga exhibition had come from Lady Ivy Chamberlain, widow of Lord Austen Chamberlain and sister-in-law of the British Prime Minister, Neville Chamberlain. She described Zuloaga as 'perhaps the greatest of Spain's modern painters'.[14] Supporting the idea the Duke of Alba wrote to Conde de Jordana, deputy head of government and Minister of Foreign Affairs, saying that it 'would serve us greatly as propaganda, since, as is natural, everything will be done in the Nationalist Spain, and the proceeds will be destined for the needy in the liberated zone'.[15] The London exhibition followed a presentation of 29 paintings by Zuloaga at the Venice Biennale in the summer of 1938 as a showcase promoting the traditional values of Nationalist Spain.[16] Privately Zuloaga was frank about the propangandist intentions of his exhibition, declaring to his American patron Alice Garrett:

> my show closes after tomorrow and here's the result. Great success among artists. Good success with the press and terrible success in sales. My show has become an issue of politics, because, since 80% of the English are on the side of the reds in Spain; that is to say – anti-Franco, they've burned me. I should tell you that I don't care because on the other hand I've made an enormous propaganda for our Spain, the Spain of Franco – and that makes me happier than anything.[17]

In public Zuloaga was not so vocal about the war, instead letting the paintings featuring women in mantillas, bullfights and conservative portraits convey their own message. Indeed the reviewer of the *Catholic Herald* recorded that:

> Ignacio Zuloaga, painter, bullfighter, ardent Spanish nationalist, standing in front of his most flamboyant canvas representing a flaming Alcázar, refused to discuss his country's war, much in the same way as he had refused to discuss his work. Of the war he said it was too terrible. 'There is nothing to add, but I can only say that I believe soon it will be over now', he said.[18]

FIG. 22
EL GRECO (1541–1614)
The Opening of the Fifth Seal
c.1608–14
Oil on canvas
224.5 x 192.8 cm
Metropolitan Museum
of Art, New York

In addition to his own work Lady Chamberlain had persuaded Zuloaga to include one of his significant collection of paintings by El Greco, *The Opening of the Fifth Seal* (figs. 22) (also known as *Profane Love*), which was the most important example of the artist's work seen in London for several years.[19] Its presentation led the reviewer of the *Catholic Herald* to declare: 'I can assure the reader that a visit to the Exhibition is very well worth-while – and if I have any suspicious readers who think that real art can only come from the Left progressives, let me remind them that there is also a hitherto un-exhibited El Greco to see.'[20] El Greco had come to be viewed as a forerunner of the modern movement, and *The Opening of the Fifth Seal* had been a key influence, such as on Picasso's *Demoiselles d'Avignon* (1907, Museum of Modern Art) – Picasso saw the El Greco in Zuloaga's Paris studio. Yet, just as El Greco's views of Toledo were a reference point for Zuloaga's burning Alcázar, his imagery was equally utilised by Republican supporters, for example in E. McKnight Kauffer's poster for Spanish medical

FIG. 23
FRANCISCO DE GOYA
(1746–1828)
'Madre Infeliz!
(Unhappy Mother!)' from
The Disasters of War 1810–20
published 1863
Etching, burnished aquatint
and drypoint on wove paper
17.4 x 12.8 cm
Lent by David Scrase

FIG. 24
FRANCISCO DE GOYA
(1746–1828)
'*Nada el lo dirá
(Nothing -The Event will Tell)*',
from *the Disasters of War*
1810–20
published 1863
Etching, burnished aquatint,
lavis, drypoint and burin on
wove paper
19.6 x 14.5 cm
Lent by David Scrase

aid (fig. 76), and as a point of reference for artists such as Ursula McCannell (figs. 130–2).

Another claim by the Nationalists, that the Republicans had sold all the works in the Prado by Goya to the Soviet Union, was discredited in part by an exhibition of the artist's works held at the Victoria and Albert Museum in July 1938. Pérez Rubio had brought 40 original drawings for Goya's *Caprichos* from the Prado Museum collection to the Spanish embassy in London, as well as the etching suites *Los Proverbios* (also known as *The Dispirates*, 1819–24), *Los Caprichos* (1797–8) and *La Tauromanquia* (1816). In addition, he brought over a seventh and final edition of *Los Desastres de la Guerra* (*The Disasters of War*). These were of particular significance as they provided a historic parallel to the contemporary conflict, having been created in response to the Spanish Peninsula Wars of 1808–14, and now serving as a highly relevant inspiration to contemporary artists, for example Picasso's etchings *The Dream and Life of Franco* (fig. 117). The series featured unflinching depictions of many of the atrocities of war,

including mutilation, torture and rape (see figs. 23, 24, 26). They were seen as a powerful comment on the barbarity of war and a testament to what Goya had described as '*el desmembramiento d'España*' – the dismemberment of Spain. Adolfo Rupérez had printed 150 sets of the etchings from the original plates in the collection of the Academy of Fine Arts of San Fernando, with three sets dedicated to Stalin, Eleanor Roosevelt, and the Republican President, Azcaña.[21] The British printmaker and Surrealist S.W. Hayter had seen the plates being printed in the Calcografia Madrid when he visited the city in autumn 1937, and wrote to Arthur Wesley Wheen at the V&A to introduce Pérez Rubio, saying that he was 'a good friend of mine' and asking 'if you can help him in any way I would be most grateful'.[22] Meeting with James Laver, Keeper of the Department of Engraving, Illustration and Design, on 2 June 1938 Pérez Rubio put forward a proposal for an exhibition of the Goyas and was 'extremely anxious' to hold the exhibition at the V&A rather than at a private gallery and 'to arrange for the material to be exhibited

FIG. 25
LAWRENCE GOWING
(1918–91)
Non-Combatant 5th May (After Goya) c.1938
Oil on canvas
The Faringdon
Collection Trust

FIG. 26
FRANCISCO DE GOYA
(1746–1828)
'De qué sirve una taza
(What Good is a Single Cup?)'
from *The Disasters of War*
1810–20
published 1863
Etching, burnished aquatint
and lavis on wove paper
17.9 x 12.6 cm
Lent by David Scrase

Maclagan's opinion is that the proposal is an attractive one and that such an exhibition would have a strong topical and artistic interest; but we feel that the political issues involved make it necessary to ask your opinion whether there would be any objection to the use of the Museum for an exhibition of this nature, which would inevitably have, or might be represented to have, a propagandist intention.[26]

Gaselee's response was supportive, but mindful of any possibility of it being interpreted as partisan:

We cannot see that the holding of this exhibition could be interpreted as propaganda for either side in the Spanish civil war, and we have no doubt that Maclagan will be able to ensure that the advertisements and catalogues of the exhibition shall not contain anything of a propagandist nature. We attach some importance to this, and we would not like printed documents to go out which the Nationalists could seize upon as evidence of a British Governmental bias opposed to them, and therefore in conflict with our policy of non-intervention.[27]

In a memorandum Maclagan referred to Laver's proposal to also exhibit a contemporary etching 'representing damage done by bombs in the immediate neighbourhood of the office in which the plates were being printed', but told him that Gaselee would 'see strong objections' to this being exhibited. He also mentioned that, whilst their poster and broadsheet had to be kept free from anything that might be called propaganda, Gaselee 'would not boggle at the likelihood of the English "left" papers making propagandist, use of the show'.[28]

The exhibition took place from July to September 1938 and, despite the above provisions, Goya's works were reproduced in both the Republican press *(El Mono Azul, Voz de París, ABC, Tiempos Nuevos, Nosotros)* as well as the insurgent *(Vértice)*. It provided an opportunity to counter negative propaganda from the Nationalists that the Republicans were destroying churches and

with the least possible delay'.[23] In the minutes of the Exhibition Department meeting dated 3 June 1938, Eric Maclagan, Director of the V&A, commented:

From the artistic point of view such an Exhibition would be of real importance [...] And as many of the etchings deal with the horrors of war, the Exhibition would have a strong topical interest as well. For these reasons I should in normal circumstances have welcomed the suggestion, and the space involved would not in any case be considerable. [...] But the political issues involved are so important that they must decide our acceptance or rejection of the proposal.[24]

The minutes proceeded to record that, 'Señor Rubio admitted his hope that such an Exhibition would convince British people that the Government of Spain did not consist entirely of barbarians',[25] and a further note to consult the Foreign Office on the proposal. In a subsequent cautious letter to the diplomat Sir Stephen Gaselee at the Foreign Office, W.H. Richardson of the V&A wrote:

art treasures, and for them to discuss their cultural strategy – which involved creating an inventory of all the works of art in loyalist Spain and preventing the export sale of cultural items, and which apparently included the discovery of 53 previously unknown Goyas in private collections. Pérez Rubio spoke of how: 'These are the last disasters of the first war, and now we are going through the first disasters of the last war.'[29] On 30 July 1938 an article titled 'Insurgents Object to London Exhibition' appeared in the *Evening Standard*, reporting that the Nationalist Fine Arts Department in Burgos had issued a statement complaining of the Goya exhibition and alleging that the engravings were produced 'at the cost of the Reds spoiling, with the complicity of artists and technicians, the Goya plates which were kept at the Academy of Fine Arts of San Fernando in Madrid'.[30] Because the V&A had presented the Goya exhibition the Spanish Nationalists initially refused to allow Michael Stewart, Assistant Keeper in Architecture and Sculpture at the V&A,[31] permission to travel in Nationalist Spain to see works of art. Commenting on this in a letter to Maclagan, Gaselee observed: 'The foolish people have taken as a sign of political sympathy what you and I know was a purely artistic movement.'[32] However, this delay is as much likely to have been due to the Nationalists' concern about Stewart recording the state of their *Servicio Artistico de Vanguardia* (Front-line Artistic Service). The Director Pedro Murguruza was to write internally of delaying the visit, 'thus avoiding [Stewart] seeing the disgraceful spectacle of the state of abandonment in which our National Artistic Treasures currently lie...'[33]

Another timely exhibition of Spanish art, entitled *From Greco to Goya*, was held in London at the Spanish Art Gallery in Chesterfield Gardens. In addition to paintings by Ribera, Velásquez, Zurbarán, and Murillo, it also featured a set of Goya's *Disasters of War*. The *British Journal of Nursing* recorded that it raised £512 5s 2d for the British Red Cross Society's Spanish Relief Fund.[34] The *Burlington Magazine* noted that, 'it is not often that it falls to the lots of a reviewer of an exhibition in aid of charity to notice an assemblage of such interest and importance as the one now brought together by Messrs. Tomas Harris in their new gallery at 6 Chesterfield Gardens – a collection which will live long in the memory of those

privileged to see it.'[35] Such presentations brought the work of Goya to new audiences in Britain, and whilst the savagery of his images was to subtly influence the macabre works of Edward Burra, the Spanish artist was also a direct point of reference for the Realists, including several members of the Euston Road School (formed by William Coldstream, Victor Pasmore and Claude Rogers in 1937, and strongly affiliated to the Artists International Association). The largely socialist members asserted the importance of painting traditional subjects in a figurative manner and sought to create a widely understandable and socially relevant art. For the 1939 May Day Procession in London the artists Graham Bell, Rodrigo Moynihan and others created a series of banners featuring transcriptions of the *Disasters of War*.[36] Lawrence Gowing, who was to be a conscientious objector in the Second World War, also produced an oil painting titled *Non-Combatant 5th May (after Goya)* (fig. 25), which was bought by Lord Faringdon, a leading supporter of the Republican cause.

In a civil war characterised by immense brutality, in which there were around 500,000 casualties, the question of *care* for Spain's cultural patrimony was central to the battle of propaganda. The involvement of the British art world in assessing each faction's attempts to safeguard their artistic treasures, and in presenting exhibitions of historic Spanish art in Britain, was not insubstantial. The contemporary relevance of exhibitions of Goya and El Greco further affirmed the notion that culture was another front of the war, as had been noted in relation to the exhibitions of Picasso's *Guernica*. Musing on this, Zervos and Penrose were poignantly to note in their book on Catalan art in 1937:

> the struggle of the Spanish Civil War is symptomatic of the moral crisis through which society in general is passing. If the creations of the human spirit are to be preserved and a closer link formed between them and our everyday lives the example of the revolutionaries of Catalonia, who have recognised the value of the art of their ancestors and sought to bring it more closely into contact with the life of the people, should serve as an encouragement to those who have faith in humanity.[37]

1. An English edition was printed at the end of October 1936, possibly financed by the Nationalist sympathisers Sir Charles Petrie and Douglas Jerrold, friends of the representative of the Burgos Junta, the Marqués de Merry del Valand. See García 2010, p.35.

2. García, *ibid*, p.159.

3. García, *ibid*, p.159.

4. Gascoyne recorded in his *Journal 1936–37* (London: Enitharmon Press, 1997) that Miravittles was later to be shot by the Francoists at the end of the war, but in fact he went into extended exile from 1939 until 1963. For more information on Miravitlles see Enric Pujol, 'Jaume Miravitlles and Marxism: a Twentieth-Century Voyage', *Journal of Catalan Intellectual History*, issue 3, 2012, pp 29–45.

5. Gascoyne, *ibid*, p.44.

6. Zervos and Penrose, in Zervos 1937, p.28.

7. Zervos, *ibid*, p.29.

8. Penrose 1981, p.84.

9. García suggests that the main purpose of this was to keep these at hand 'should it ever be necessary to dispose of them in order to raise funds'. See García, *ibid*, p.159.

10. Àlvarez Lopera, José quoted in García, p.162.

11. 'Spain and its Art Treasures: Government's Care for Paintings', *Daily Telegraph*, 21 August 1937.

12. See García, *ibid*, p.161

13. The *Guernica* exhibition took place from 4 to 29 October and the Zuloaga from 10 December 1938 to 5 January 1939. Roland Penrose records that 'the larger of the two rooms had been booked previously by Franco's supporters for an exhibition of an enormous painting by Zuloaga in honour of the fascist defenders of the Alcázar in Toledo, but it was a pleasure to Picasso's friends to see the great room more frequented by cats than human visitors, while *Guernica* was daily attracting crowds' (Roland Penrose, *Scrapbook*, p.87). Herschel B. Chipp and Jonathan Richardson both suggest that the exhibitions were concurrent. See Herschel B. Chipp *Picasso's Guernica* (Berkeley: University of California Press, 1988), footnote 1, p.219 and Richardson's *Life of Picasso Vol. 1* (London: Jonanthan Cape, 1991), p.430: 'When London's New Burlington Gallery exhibited *Guernica* in 1938, it also exhibited Zuloaga's riposte to it – a melodramatic commemoration of the *Defenders of the Alcazar of Toledo*. The *Guernica* room was always full; the Toledo one always empty.'

14. Lady Ivy Chamberlain, *Ignacio Zuloaga catalogue* (London: New Burlington Galleries, 1938).

15. García, *ibid*, p.62.

16. For more information see Dena Crosson, 'Ignacio Zuloaga and the Problem of Spain', PhD 2009, University of Maryland.

17. Evergreen Foundation, *Zuloaga/Garret Correspondence*, Baltimore, 4 January 1939.

18. 'Pictures by Zuloaga', *Catholic Herald*, 16 December 1938.

19. Zuloaga had been partly responsible for reviving interest in El Greco's work. The painting had been owned by Antonio Cánovas del Castillo, the former Prime Minister of Spain, and Zuloaga bought it from Rafael Vázquez de la Plaza. It was subsequently sold by the Zuloaga Museum to the Metropolitan Museum in New York.

20. *Catholic Herald*, *ibid*.

21. At the same time the Comissariat de Propaganda de la Generalitat de Catalunya published Ramón Xuriguera's monograph *Goya, pintor del pueblo* (Goya, Painter of the People).

22. Handwritten note from S.W. Hayter in V&A Archives. I am grateful to Christopher Marsden for his assistance in providing access to the V&A archives relating to this episode.

23. Minutes of the Exhibition Departmental Meeting, Eric MacLagan, 3 June 1938, V&A Archives. James Laver was Director of Art Classes at the Working Men's College in Camden Town from 1926 to 1938, and co-presented the first television series on the history of fashion with the left-wing artist Pearl Binder in 1937.

24. *Ibid*.

25. *Ibid*.

26. Letter from W.H. Richardson to Stephen Gaselee at the Foreign Office, 8 June 1938. V&A Archives.

27. Letter from Stephen Gaselee of the Foreign Office to W.H. Richardson, 17 June 1938. V&A Archives.

28. Minute by Eric MacLagan, Board of Education, 20 June 1938, V&A Archives.

29. Pérez Rubio quoted in 'Goya's Engravings Published in Wartime Madrid', *Singapore Free Press and Mercantile Advertisers*, 27 June 1938, p.7.

30. *Evening Standard*, 30 July 1938, V&A Archives.

31. Michael Stewart had previously been in the department of Engraving, Illustration and Design and was later a diplomat and knighted, serving as ambassador in Athens.

32. Letter from Stephen Gaselee to Eric Maclagan, 1 September 1938. V&A Archives. The Spanish politician and former Prime Minister Don Álvaro de Figueroa, Count of Romanoes, wrote to *The Times* on 1 September 1938. The ambassador replied, avoiding the need for the V&A to make any direct statement or response.

33. Murguruza, quoted in García, *ibid*, p.164. Stewart eventually visited in January 1939 and wrote a favourable report, which was published in *The Times*.

34. *British Journal of Nursing*, February 1939, p.52.

35. *Burlington Magazine*, December 1938, vol.73, no.429.

36. These banners no longer exist, having apparently been confiscated by the Home Guard during the Second World War.

37. Zervos, *ibid*, p.36.

2 ARTISTS TAKE SIDES: The Artists International Association and Support for Spain

The Spanish Civil War threw into stark relief the fundamental question of the nature of the artist's role within society and their engagement with politics. Julian Trevelyan was to recall that, 'until the Spanish War started in 1936, there was an air of gentle frivolity about our life in London. True, the Hitler terror had begun, and refugees were pouring into England. Moreover it was clear from Abyssinia and Japan that war and violence were to be the order of the day', but after the outbreak of the Civil War 'for the next three years our thoughts and consciences were turned to Spain'.[1]

In fact, the polarisation of international politics during the 1930s had been reflected in the increased political engagement of artists, particularly by those concerned by the rise of Nazism in Germany and Italian fascism. In the autumn of 1933 the Artists International Association (AIA) had been formed by a group of left-wing artists including Clifford Rowe, Misha Black, Pearl Binder, Peggy Angus and 'the three James' – James Boswell, James Fitton and James Holland. In their first published statement in 1934 the AIA declared that it was their aim to mobilise 'the International Unity of Artists Against Imperialist War on the Soviet Union, Fascism and Colonial Oppression'. Over the subsequent years they inaugurated a series of exhibitions on 'a central theme'. These included *The Social Scene* in 1934, presenting artworks that depicted the 'Social Conditions and Struggles of Today', and *Artists Against Fascism and War* held in Soho Square in November 1935, which characterised the AIA's identity as a 'United Front Against Fascism and War' and attracted more than 6,000 visitors.

By the outbreak of the Spanish Civil War in July 1936 the AIA had over 600 members, ranging from major figures of the London art establishment such as Augustus John, Stanley Spencer, Eric Gill, Vanessa Bell and Duncan Grant, to a younger generation of modernists including Henry Moore, Barbara Hepworth, John Piper and Ben Nicholson, as well as many little-known 'commercial' artists – designers and illustrators, art teachers and students. During the 1930s the membership crossed the spectrum of artistic styles and movements from Royal Academicians to members of the London Group,

Circle, the Euston Road Group and the British Surrealists. The prime focus was initially propaganda, reflecting the fact that the core members of the AIA were committed communists. Indeed, several had visited the USSR in the early 1930s including Peggy Angus, Pearl Binder, Betty Rea and Clifford Rowe.

There was a close link between the AIA and the magazine *Left Review,* which ran from October 1934 to May 1938, providing a monthly review of poetry, short stories, reviews and opinion pieces. The editors of the magazine included Montague Slater, Tom Wintringham (who was to become Commander of the British Battalion of the International Brigades), Alick West and Randall Swingler, and it featured contributions from the likes of Berthold Brecht, Eric Gill, Pablo Neruda, Paul Robeson, George Bernard Shaw and J.B. Priestley. James Boswell was appointed as the art editor and, together with Fitton and Holland, he shaped the distinctive style of the magazine's satirical cartoons, with occasional contributions from illustrators and cartoonists such as Pearl Binder and Clare Leighton. Boswell's satirical illustrations in *Left Review* and the *Daily Worker* show a debt to German artists George Grosz and Otto Dix – as in cartoons like *What! Not Murdered the Spanish Workers Yet?* (fig. 30) signed under the name 'Buchan' (a shortened version of his middle name Buchanon), in which Franco is presented as the heir to Hitler and Mussolini's violent actions against the workers. The fight against fascism was a frequent theme of cartoons such as Binder's *Chalking Squad* (fig. 29), in which a flat-capped worker keeps his eye out for an approaching policeman whilst his female accomplice chalks the slogan 'WORKERS UNITE AGAINST FASCISM' on a wall. The May 1935 issue featured a collage by 'Luke' (fig. 31) with a photograph of Oswald Mosley gesticulating during a public rally inserted into the lap of a chimpanzee with its arm raised in the same gesture.

Several members of the AIA took to the streets of London to directly oppose Mosley and his 'Blackshirts'. Artist Reg Turner recalled how he and other students at the Royal College who had joined the AIA were:

FIG. 28
JAMES BOSWELL (1906–71)
*Speaker's Corner
(with Bonner Thompson)*
1938
Lithograph on paper
21.6 x 20.3 cm
Ron Heisler Collection

convinced anti-Fascists and we were all deeply involved in anti-Mosley work. Artists seemed to go to political organisations in those days, to Anarchist groups, Communist Party groups, Socialist groups, Labour League of Youth, and all that kind of thing. The factor that kept us together was the anti-Fascist business and the Civil War in Spain … however varied we were in work or outlook.[2]

Turner and other artists got involved in organised opposition at Mosley's huge fascist demonstration at Olympia (where Turner got several cracked ribs), and at the infamous Cable Street Battle on 4 October 1936 where 2–3,000 Blackshirts attempted to march through a predominantly Jewish area in the East End of London. They were opposed by 100,000 anti-fascist protesters, who clashed with the 6,000 policemen trying to clear the road.

Felicia Browne was to become a potent symbol of the fight against fascism, for which she paid the ultimate sacrifice. Browne was not only the first of more than 500 British volunteers to

FIG. 29
PEARL BINDER (1904–90)
Chalking Squad 1935
Drawing, reproduced
in *Left Review*
Collection of Ruth Boswell

FIG. 30
JAMES BOSWELL (1906–71)
*What! Not Murdered the
Spanish Workers Yet?* 1936
Drawing reproduced in *Left
Review*, September 1936
Collection of Ruth Boswell

FIG. 31
'LUKE'
'Mosley', collage for
Left Review, May 1935
Collage on paper
37 x 24 cm
Austin / Desmond Fine Ar

FIG. 32
Cover for Oswald Mosley's
Tomorrow We Live 1938
London, Greater Britain
Publications
The Sherwin Collection

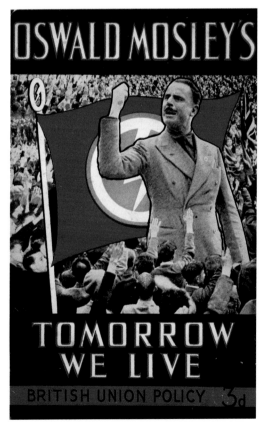

die in battle, but she was also the only British woman to play a combatant role in the conflict. She had studied at the Slade School of Art in the 1920s, where she was a contemporary of William Coldstream, Clive Branson, Claude Rogers and Nan Youngman. In 1928 she moved to Berlin where she trained as a stone carver, witnessing the rise of Nazism and apparently spending her money on helping friends flee Germany. Returning to Britain in 1933 she had joined the Communist Party and the newly founded AIA, visiting the Soviet Union, Hungary and Czechoslovakia. Browne's evident skills as an artist are revealed in her poignant, searching *Self-Portrait* (fig. 33).

In 1936 Browne obtained a pass as a journalistic assistant to Edith Bone, who had started working with *Daily Worker* correspondent Claud Cockburn (under the pseudonym Frank Pitcairn). Heading to Spain in July, perhaps for the People's Olympiad which was organised as a riposte to the Munich Olympics held in Nazi Germany, Browne and Bone were caught up in the violence that accompanied the outbreak of the war. Whilst near Lérida Browne was picked up by a car full of anarchists and she made drawings of members of the militia (see fig.34). According to the *Daily Express* correspondent Sidney Smith she had gone to the communist militia office on 3 August and demanded to be enlisted to fight on the Saragossa front, declaring that, 'I am a member of the London Communists and can fight as well as any man'.[3] Her final letter to her friend the artist Elizabeth Watson, on 7 August, records that the volunteers had 'nothing to do but hang around until we get somewhere; no uniforms or rifles so everybody looks like pirates', and that they were cooked food by 'enormous cubic women' in the filthy barracks (possibly the subject of her drawings of Spanish women; fig. 34). In late August she was one of a party sent to blow up a rebel munitions train, and when they came under fire from a party of fascists she went forward to give an Italian comrade first aid. 'When she reached him, the Fascists directed their united fire against the two of them. With several wounds in the breast and one in the back, Felicia, our brave fighter in the cause of Freedom, sank dead to the ground.'[4]

Browne's body had to be left there by her comrades, but amongst her possessions they retrieved her sketchbook filled with drawings of her fellow militia. The sketchbook reached Tom Wintringham in Barcelona, who at the time was working as a journalist for the *Daily Worker*. He suggested to Harry Pollitt, leader of the British Communist Party, that the sketches be sold by the AIA to raise money for Spanish relief. In October 1936 an exhibition of her drawings was held in Frith Street in London, featuring 30 drawings of Spanish subjects as well as others she had produced in Germany, Hungary, Russia and Czechoslovakia in the earlier 1930s – with a catalogue text by Duncan Grant and a memorial publication of her drawings that was published by Lawrence & Wishart to raise money for the Spanish Medical Aid Committee.[5] The reviewer of the *New Statesman* noted that the absence of:

all sentimentality, all propaganda, all effort to be 'proletarian' deserves the consideration of those who fancy that it is an artist's business

FIG. 33
FELICIA BROWNE (1904–36)
Self Portrait n.d
Oil on canvas
33 x 23 cm
Private Collection

FIG. 34
FELICIA BROWNE (1904–36)
Drawings of Spanish Militiamen and women, reproduced in *Drawings* by Felicia Browne, Lawrence & Wishart, London 1936
Private Collection

to use his art for the expression of his political beliefs. Miss Felicia Browne was under no such delusion. When she drew she was content to draw as well as in her lay. And as for her convictions – she showed these by dying for them.[6]

Browne was presented by the AIA as the epitome of an artist who had made a noble choice in favour of direct political action. The memorial publication featured a quote from a letter she had written to Watson in spring 1936, in which she was discussing her choice to work as a scullion in a teashop, in order to suggest that she had made a choice between making art and political commitment in Spain:

You say I am escaping or evading things by not painting or making sculpture. If there is no painting or sculpture to be made, I cannot make it. I can only *make* out what is valid and urgent to me. If painting or sculpture were more urgent or valid to me than the

JOHN CORNFORD

John Cornford, a Cambridge student, was one of the first Englishmen to volunteer for the International Brigade. His life was an example for our generation.

Killed fighting Fascism in Spain, on 28th December 1936, at the age of 21

A MEMORIAL VOLUME

TWO AND SIXPENCE

FIG. 35
Poets Stephen Spender, George Green (fourth and fifth from left), Ewart Milne (left) and artist Wogan Phillips (second left) driving ambulances from Barcelona to Valencia, 1937
Photograph, International Brigade Archive at the Marx Memorial Library

FIG. 36
Cover of *John Cornford: A Memorial Volume*, 1938

FIG. 37
Ramsey and Muspratt
(Lettice Ramsey; 1895–1985)
and Helen Muspratt;
1907–2001)
'The Islanders', Photograph of
John Cornford and Ray Peters,
1934,
Bromide print, 30.3 × 36.2cm,
Private collection

earthquake which is happening in the revolution, or if these two were reconciled, so that the demands of the one didn't conflict (in time even or concentration) with the demands of the other, I should paint or make sculpture.[7]

Felicia Browne's direct engagement had a particular resonance for other female artists. As Nan Youngman was to declare, 'Felicia Browne's death was the thing that brought me into the AIA'.[8] Browne was to artists what the subsequent death of the poet John Cornford was to writers and to literature. Cornford had joined the Communist Party of Great Britain whilst an undergraduate at Cambridge. In 1936 he travelled to Spain, briefly serving with the P.O.U.M. (Workers' Party of Marxist Unification) militia before returning to England to recruit volunteers and travelling with them to Spain, where they joined the International Brigades. After fighting in the defence of Madrid, Cornford was killed at Lopera near Córdoba on his 21st birthday in December 1936. He was to become the ultimate romantic hero, an image shaped in

part by Ramsey and Muspratt's iconic photograph of him and his former partner Ray Peters (fig. 37) and by a memorial volume published in 1938 (fig.36), featuring a photograph by Communist spy Michael Straight. It was reviewed by Stephen Spender who observed that, 'Cornford's life speaks for itself in a way that burns the imagination ... The fact that Cornford lived and that others like him still live, is an important lesson to the leaders of democracies. It shows that people will live and die and fight for democracy if it gives them the justice and freedom which are worth fighting for'.[9]

There is an apocryphal story that the leader of the British Communist Party, Harry Pollitt, when encouraging Spender to join the International Brigades, told him 'to go and get killed; we need a Byron in the movement'.[10] Yet although Spender went to Spain in 1937, joining Wogan Phillips to drive an ambulance from Barcelona to Valencia (figs. 35 and 75) and taking part in the International Writers Congress, he did not fight, and in fact went to great lengths to rescue his former lover Jimmy Hyndman after he deserted from the International

Brigades.[11] The question of whether it was better to fight or to further the cause through artistic activities was a source of much discussion. Eric Ravilious wrote to his lover Helen Binyon that, 'we can pledge ourselves to fight in the event of a class war here like the one in Spain … More to the point, we can assist by design and drawings for the rather bad leaflets and such that are produced and this I mean to do if I can later.'[12] William Coldstream, discussing the fact that W.H. Auden had departed for Spain in January 1937 driving an ambulance, declared to his friend Dr John Rake: 'You must not be depressed by people like him going to Spain. I talked for hours with him over it … Thank God he will never be a fanatic anyway … Poets are all such good characters and so responsible. Painters are mostly bad characters and without principles so perhaps I have a chance.'[13] After a visit from Elizabeth Watson, Vanessa Bell wrote to her son, the poet Julian Bell, of Browne's death – in an attempt to encourage him not to fight in Spain and instead use his creative skills to support the cause:

So she was killed, which does seem a terrible waste of someone gifted, as she evidently was. I understood your wanting to go and see what war was like, and perhaps I should understand your wanting to go to Spain if you were here, only I do think nearly all war is madness. It's destruction and not creation, and it's mad to destroy the best things and people in the world, if one can anyhow avoid it. You object to cutting down trees. Isn't war that, a million times worse? I see one couldn't help joining anti-fascists if fascists started attacking, as they have in Spain. But I think you and other young people, who are the only hope of the world for the next 40 or 50 years, can do much more to help by not going out of your way to be shot. Of course going as a war correspondent is different, but I am glad, my dear that I don't have to try to reconcile myself to your rushing off to Spain. I think though, if it were necessary, I could find plenty of arguments against your doing so, but I wonder if they'd prevail.[14]

At the request of Dr Janet Vaughan, a member of the Spanish Medical Aid Committee, Duncan Grant, Vanessa Bell, her son Quentin and daughter Angelica had designed posters advertising a public meeting to raise money to send medical help to Spain.[15] Bell complained of AIA committee meetings and how:

> the difficulty was not to get all the work put on to oneself – this sounds very conceited and may only be my view – but I resisted firmly. Duncan has lent them his studio for 2 meetings which I considered weak. But I see we may both inevitably be on the selecting com. [sic] for the show which will be difficult and tiresome. It's a hopeless mixture of politics and art I think – they can't be mixed.[16]

In subsequent letters to Julian, Vanessa did her best to dissuade him from active combat but instead to provide support in different ways as she and others were doing:

I feel strongly that if you want really to do what is best for the world and not only what would relieve your own feelings most at the moment, it is clearly better to help by thinking, writing, speaking, planning, rather than action in the field. You would be one of many in action, no more and no less valuable, but you have a better intelligence than most people, and so it should be used, and not destroyed by a chance bullet. This really isn't because I should mind it. I feel exactly the same about anyone who has brains above the average. It is I think the only hope of the world that such people make themselves felt. Don't think I don't understand and sympathise with your feelings about helping Spain and using your talents as a soldier – which I am quite ready to believe in. Only if they exist, surely my dear you should have gone into the army! If you went to Spain, not knowing the language or the people or the country and its conditions, you could only have gone into the army as other foreigners have done and been used by those in command. That is the worst

FIG. 42
Harry Pollitt, leader of the British Communist Party, at the Ebro front in Spain holding the International Brigade Banner, Christmas 1937.
The banner was made by the AIA (designed by James Lucas and embroidered by Phyllis Ladyman, with a carved fist finial by Betty Rea) International Brigade Archive at the Marx Memorial Library (Box A2: A/50E)

of going to fight. You *must* become part of a machine and do what someone else thinks you ought to do. No one nowadays could become a general at once and decide on strategy, etc, and you'd only have to help to carry out what might seem to you a quite wrong policy. Isn't this so? In fact, in Spain, I suppose it's been want of arms that has prevented the government from winning, and that you couldn't have helped....[17]

Despite his mother's attempts to dissuade him, Julian Bell was convinced of the need to go to Spain and wrote of 'the usefulness of war experience in the future and the prestige one would gain in literature and – even more – Left politics'.[18] Previously, in 1935, he had edited a collection of essays written by conscientious objectors called *We Did Not Fight* in which, despite it being predominantly pacifist in viewpoint, he had allowed for some situations that called for force:

> In such a situation the most active and ardent war resisters – at least among my generation,

those of military age – are more likely to take the line of revolutionary action than conscientious objection. This is not to say that more than a small minority of us are communists, or even socialists. But those of us who care about the human race and what happens to it have come to believe that only effective action counts... I believe that the war-resistance movements of my generation will in the end succeed in putting down war – by force if necessary.[19]

Although his family dissuaded him from joining the International Brigades, Bell was resolved to work as an ambulance driver with the British Medical Aid Unit. He left for Spain on 6 June 1937 and served with the 35th Division Medical Service in El Escorial, and subsequently at Villanueva de la Cañada. After his ambulance was destroyed by a bomb Bell volunteered as a stretcher-bearer and was put in charge of 30 men. On 18 July he was driving a replacement lorry to fill in the shell-holes that pitted the road to the front, when it came under attack from a Nationalist

FIG. 43
CLIVE BRANSON (1907–44)
Demonstration In Battersea
1939
Oil on canvas
40 x 60 cm
Collection of Rosa Branson

bomber aircraft. He sought shelter under the vehicle, but died later from shrapnel injuries and was buried in the cemetery at Fuencarral, north of Madrid. On learning the news Vanessa Bell suffered a breakdown. Through a sad irony, on the evening that Grant went to tell Angelica of her brother's death she was dancing in a ballet based on Goya's print series, *The Disasters of War.*

Just days before his brother Julian's death, on 14 July 1937 Quentin Bell painted *May Day Procession with Banners* (fig. 38). This painting recorded the intensity of feeling at the annual workers' protest – a sea of red flags and political banners in support of left-wing causes and Republican Spain.[20] The picture captured the potent atmosphere of these protests in the late 1930s, at which organisations such as the AIA played an active role. As Reg Turner was to recall:

> all these groups would come together for the massive May Day demonstrations. Big groups of artists would be formed to make the decorations for these festivals, making banners and floats; there would be as many

as several hundred of us combined together. Nothing survived, everything went into the dustbin entirely. We gave up our time to help organise the decorations for these demonstrations, instead of doing paintings, then we did illustrations for the Young Communist League newspaper, the Labour League of Youth paper and things like that.[21]

The final issue of *Left Review* in May 1938 was dedicated to May Day, and included messages from the artist Eric Gill, the scientist J.B.S. Haldane, the actress Sybil Thorndike, the Dean of Canterbury Cathedral, and the playwright Sean O'Casey. There were apparently around 200 artists marching on May Day 1938. One group including Richard Carline, Irina Moore and the poet Kathleen Raine marched under a banner with the William Blake quote 'A WARLIKE STATE CANNOT CREATE', whilst behind them marched architects around a banner declaring 'ARCHITECTS FOR SOCIALISM AND A PLANNED SOCIETY'. Famously, four members of the Surrealist group dressed as Prime Minister Neville Chamberlain in masks by F.E. McWilliam, shouting

FIG. 44
CLIVE BRANSON (1907–44)
Daily Worker (July 22) 1939
Oil on canvas laid on board
34.5 x 24.5 cm
Collection of Rosa Branson

FIG. 45
CLIVE BRANSON (1907–44)
Noreen and Rosa
January 1940
Oil on canvas
50.5 x 40 cm
Collection of Rosa Branson

'Chamberlain must Go!', followed by an ice-cream tricycle with a wire-netting structure filled with coloured balloons and topped with a horse's head made by Julian Trevelyan (see chapter 5).

The AIA provided a banner for the British Battalion of the International Brigades, featuring a star and the emblem of the clenched fist (the symbol of resistance to fascism) with the words 'FREEDOM DEMOCRACY PEACE' on a red background (fig. 42). It was designed by James Lucas and embroidered by his wife Phyllis Ladyman, with a banner pole also featuring a clenched fist that was sculpted by Betty Rea. The original was captured in battle. A copy was made in 1938, which was sent to Spain, embroidered with the names of each of the battles in which the British Battalion served – and until the death of the last known member of the International Brigades in Britain in 2013, it was used at their funerals to cover the coffin.

Clive Branson and Hugh Slater, former contemporaries at the Slade with William Coldstream, both joined the International Brigades and went to Spain. Branson joined in spring 1937

but stayed in England to help with the travel arrangements of other volunteers (it had been made illegal to volunteer or help volunteers in January 1937) and so did not travel to Spain until January 1938, when it became clear that he was under police surveillance. He was subsequently captured after the Battle at Calaceite around 31 March 1938 whilst serving in the Major Atlee Company of the British Battalion, and imprisoned at Palencia in an Italian concentration camp, where he recorded his fellow prisoners and the camp in a series of paintings, sketches and poems (see chapter 7, fig. 133). He had not painted between 1931 and 1937 as he had given up to work for the International Labour Party and then the Communist Party, but thereafter he painted several works in a consciously naïve figurative style that recalls the work of the Ashington Art Group, a group of Northumberland miners without artistic training who became known as the Pitmen Painters for their depictions of everyday life in the 1930s. After his release in October 1938 Branson became the organiser of the International Brigade Convoy, which toured Britain raising more than £5000 for

food and medical aid for Spain. Branson and his wife Noreen (granddaughter of the Fifth Marquis of Sligo) had set up an Aid Spain committee in Battersea in 1936, organising numerous events over the next few years such as the one depicted in *Demonstration in Battersea* (fig. 43). A crowd of protesters waving Spanish and communist flags is shown in a street corner of a working-class area of South London. In a domestic scene revealing deep engagement in Spain, entitled *Noreen and Rosa* (fig. 45), Branson depicted his wife and daughter at home reading a book about Spain with the distinctive orange cover of paperbacks issued between 1936 and 1938 by the Left Book Club (LBC). Founded in 1936 by Stafford Cripps, Victor Gollancz and John Strachey, to 'help with the struggle for world peace and against fascism,' by 1939 the LBC had 57,000 members, and regular meetings of over 1,500 left discussion groups around the country.[22] Other paintings such as *Daily Worker* (fig. 44) and *Selling the Daily Worker outside Projectile Engineering Works* (fig. 111) reflected the political engagement of the working classes, and made oblique criticism of British militarism. Between

September 1939 and September 1940 a single pitch in Battersea sold 25,000 copies of the *Daily Worker*.[23]

A number of fundraising exhibitions were held in London between 1936 and 1939 attracting donations from a range of artists, although it seems that few of these artworks specifically addressed the war. These included *Artists Help Spain* in December 1936 to raise funds for a field ambulance for the International Column that had been formed to defend Madrid. Organised by 'the women of the Artists International Association' the exhibition featured works donated by leading modern British artists working in a range of artistic styles, including Edward Bawden, Vanessa Bell, Jacob Epstein, Eric Gill, Duncan Grant, Augustus John, László Moholy-Nagy, Paul Nash, Ben Nicholson, Lucien Pissarro, Eric Ravilious and others. The exhibition apparently raised enough money to pay for the ambulance plus £500 worth of supplies after just one and a half days. The 'Artist's Ambulance' set off for Spain from Trafalgar Square on 15 January 1937 (fig. 46), having been on display in Palace Yard. Another was an exhibition at Whistler's House organised

FIG. 46
Medical Supplies for the International Column from the Artists International Association, 15 Jan 1937
Black and white photograph
International Brigade Archive at the Marx Memorial Library

by the Chelsea branch of the Spanish Medical Aid Committee, which included contributions from a mixture of traditional artists such as Muirhead Bone, Sir John Lavery and Lucien Pissaro, and abstract modernists such as Ben Nicholson and Moholy-Nagy. Yet the lack of direct connection between the works exhibited and the cause they were supporting led *The Times* correspondent to remark that the exhibition might as well have been for 'distressed Ruritanian agriculturalists'.[24] Julian Trevelyan recalled that:

> there were at this time numerous exhibitions where pictures were sold for Spain, some of which I helped to organise. With Ursula I also joined a scheme by which, through our subscriptions, we became foster-parents of a Spanish orphan in an institution in Spain, and we wrote him letters. Jesus, for such was his name, replied with touching poems and was always asking for more love. At the end of the Spanish War his parents, who were Asturian miners, turned up again most fortunately.[25]

In April/May 1937 the AIA held the first British Artists' Congress and the *Exhibition for Unity of Artists for Peace, for Democracy, for Cultural Progress in aid of the Spanish Republic.* The committee included McKnight Kauffer, Eric Ravilious, Clare Leighton, Edward Wadsworth, Ethelbert White and Henry Moore, and the exhibition presented an overwhelming array of over 1000 artworks, with sections devoted to various movements including the Surrealists (see chapter 5) and Abstract artists, which included Ben Nicholson, John Piper, Jean Hélion, Moholy-Nagy, Jessica Dismorr, Ivon Hitchens and Barbara Hepworth. After receiving the catalogue of the exhibition, T.S. Eliot wrote: 'No one can object to "artists" banding themselves together for the purpose of advancing political tendencies with which they sympathise; but they can only do this as human beings, or at most as representatives of a particular movement in art: they haven't claim to speak in the name of "Art" in general.'[26]

Most of the abstract works could not have been interpreted to express any form of direct political statement, except that in their contrast to the official art in Germany or Italy they could be seen to express a form of aesthetic freedom. However, in 1938–9 Barbara Hepworth did address the conflict directly by carving a maquette in planewood for an abstract sculpture entitled *Monument to the Spanish Civil War* (fig. 14), which was to be executed in stone 20 feet high but was destroyed during the Second World War. The abstract artist Alastair Morton created a painting entitled *Spanish Civil War* (fig. 48) in which the forms of a mother and child and a man holding a rifle are reduced to areas of un-modulated colour, anticipating the language of 1960s Pop Art. These contrast with the bulky figurative qualities of *Aid Spain* (fig. 47), a sculpture of a mother and child executed in coloured concrete by Peter Peri. A one-man exhibition of his sculptures organised in June 1938 by the AIA, *London Life in Concrete*, led Anthony Blunt to claim, 'one of Peri's great achievements is that he has found a medium suitable for the kind of thing that he wants to express. He has no need for the more expensive media of bronze or marble ... Instead he has exploited concrete, a rough medium which has many advantages: it is cheap; and it can be used in several colours'.[27]

The Chairman of the British Artists' Congress was Quentin Bell, who was to be instrumental in obtaining Picasso's support for a 'Grand International Meeting' to raise funds for the Basque refugee children in the summer of 1937. In May 1937, together with Duncan Grant and Vanessa Bell, he had visited Picasso's studio at the rue des Grands-Augustins in Paris. Picasso was then working on the enormous canvas for *Guernica*, of which Vanessa Bell apparently remarked: 'C'est un peu terrible.'[28] Bell, Grant and Picasso were amongst the 11 artists and writers (including Henri Matisse, Havelock Ellis and Virginia Woolf) who wrote a letter to the editor of the *Manchester Guardian* on 17 June announcing the meeting, in which they stated:

> We, who sign this letter, are a few of the thousands of members of academic and artistic professions who have been watching with profound alarm the recent events in Spain. Our work may seem far removed from politics, and still more from war; but, widely as our activities vary, they all depend on the liberty to know, to utter, and to argue freely according to conscience. We have seen this liberty attacked in recent years; our friends and colleagues in Fascist countries have been silenced, imprisoned, or exiled. Now, in a country which has contributed in no small part to our culture, a struggle is going on before our eyes, still undecided between the attackers and the deciders of freedom.
>
> Whether we wish it or not, we cannot remain unmoved by this struggle; it is our liberty, not merely the liberty of one country, that is being attacked and defended. The advantage that we enjoy of living in freedom of thought and speech and work makes it the more incumbent on us to speak out on behalf of our friends who are in danger of losing this heritage; we cannot know that we shall not be in the same danger one day. We feel it to be of the first importance that we, and all others who prize such liberty, should express our full support for this our common cause.[29]

FIG. 48
ALASTAIR MORTON
(1910–53)
Spanish Civil War 1939
Oil on canvas
68.6 x 91.4 cm
Private Collection

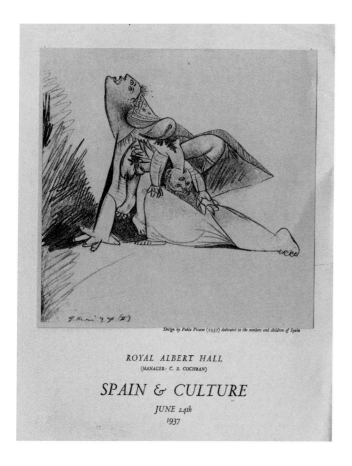

Design by Pablo Picasso (1937) dedicated to the mothers and children of Spain

ROYAL ALBERT HALL
(MANAGER: C. B. COCHRAN)

SPAIN & CULTURE

JUNE 24th
1937

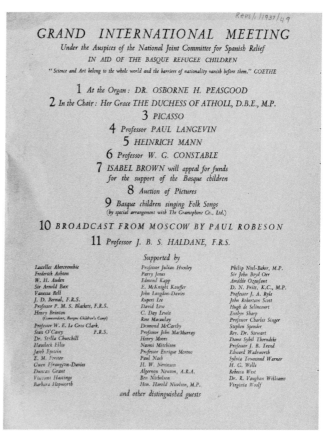

RAH/A/1937/49

GRAND INTERNATIONAL MEETING
Under the Auspices of the National Joint Committee for Spanish Relief
IN AID OF THE BASQUE REFUGEE CHILDREN
"Science and Art belong to the whole world and the barriers of nationality vanish before them." GOETHE

1 At the Organ: DR. OSBORNE H. PEASGOOD
2 In the Chair: Her Grace THE DUCHESS OF ATHOLL, D.B.E., M.P.
3 PICASSO
4 Professor PAUL LANGEVIN
5 HEINRICH MANN
6 Professor W. G. CONSTABLE
7 ISABEL BROWN will appeal for funds
for the support of the Basque children
8 Auction of Pictures
9 Basque children singing Folk Songs
(by special arrangement with The Gramophone Co., Ltd.)
10 BROADCAST FROM MOSCOW BY PAUL ROBESON
11 Professor J. B. S. HALDANE, F.R.S.

Supported by

Lascelles Abercrombie	Professor Julian Huxley	Philip Noel-Baker, M.P.
Frederick Ashton	Parry Jones	Sir John Boyd Orr
W. H. Auden	Edmond Kapp	Amédée Ozenfant
Sir Arnold Bax	E. McKnight Kauffer	D. N. Pritt, K.C., M.P.
Vanessa Bell	John Langdon-Davies	Professor J. A. Ryle
J. D. Bernal, F.R.S.	Rupert Lee	John Robertson Scott
Professor P. M. S. Blackett, F.R.S.	David Low	Hugh de Selincourt
Henry Brinton	C. Day Lewis	Evelyn Sharp
(Commandant, Basque Children's Camp)	Rose Macaulay	Professor Charles Singer
Professor W. E. Le Gros Clark	Desmond McCarthy	Stephen Spender
Sean O'Casey F.R.S.	Professor John MacMurray	Rev. Dr. Stewart
Dr. Stella Churchill	Henry Moore	Dame Sybil Thorndike
Havelock Ellis	Naomi Mitchison	Professor J. B. Trend
Jacob Epstein	Professor Enrique Moreno	Edward Wadsworth
E. M. Forster	Paul Nash	Sylvia Townsend Warner
Gwen Ffrangcon-Davies	H. W. Nevinson	H. G. Wells
Duncan Grant	Algernon Newton, A.R.A.	Rebecca West
Viscount Hastings	Ben Nicholson	Dr. R. Vaughan Williams
Barbara Hepworth	Hon. Harold Nicolson, M.P.	Virginia Woolf

and other distinguished guests

FIG. 49
Programme for the Spain and Culture Rally at the Royal Albert Hall, with a cover drawing by Pablo Picasso, June 1937
Image courtesy
Royal Albert Hall

The 'Spain and Culture' event was held at the Royal Albert Hall on 24 June 1937 under the auspices of the National Joint Committee for Spanish Relief, and chaired by Conservative MP Katherine Stewart-Murray, Duchess of Atholl. It had an illustrious list of supporters that included artists, composers, poets, scientists, philosophers and writers such as Frederick Ashton, Arnold Bax, Havelock Ellis, E.M. Forster, Viscount Hastings, Barbara Hepworth, Julian Huxley, Desmond McCarthy, Paul Nash, Ben Nicholson, Sybil Thorndike, H.G. Wells, Vaughan Williams and Virginia Woolf, amongst many others. The eminent speakers included the physicist Professor Paul Langevin, the first Director of the Courtauld Institute, the Professor W.G. Constable, and the scientist Professor J.B.S. Haldane. Many artists who attended hoped to hear Picasso speak, but in the event he was not able to attend as he was preoccupied with painting *Guernica*. Instead he gave his permission for a preliminary sketch for the mural of a mother and dead child to be reproduced on the cover of the programme, 'dedicated to the mothers and children of Spain' (fig. 49). He also donated the

drawing *Weeping Woman*, dated 16 June 1937, which was among the pictures auctioned by Isabel Brown, founder of the Spanish Medical Aid Committee, who was an impassioned fundraiser. Figurative artist William Townsend recorded in his journal that, 'our hands were smarting with applauding; but she could not sell the drawing Picasso had given, a recondite little piece of metaphysical abstraction, for which the highest bid was £80. For the programme he had made a fine drawing, agonising; for most people, to buy the other would have been no more than a gesture for the Basques'.[30] It was bought by the Picasso collector Hugh Willoughby, who exhibited it the following month with the rest of his collection at Cheltenham Museum and Art Gallery.[31]

The undeniable highlight of the evening was the presence of the African-American actor and singer Paul Robeson, who had originally been due to broadcast from Moscow, but had flown back from Russia in person as there was doubt over whether it would be sanctioned. Robeson roused the crowd by declaring that:

the artist must take sides. He must elect to fight for freedom or slavery. I have made my choice. I had no alternative. The history of the capitalist era is characterised by the degradation of my people: despoiled of their lands, their culture destroyed, they are in every country, save one, denied equal protection under the law, and deprived of their rightful place in the respect of their fellows. May your inspiring message reach every man, woman, and child who stands for freedom and justice. For the liberation of Spain from the oppression of fascist reactionaries is not a private matter of the Spaniards, but the common cause of all advanced and progressive humanity.[32]

The audience was enraptured by the significance of Robeson's words. Townsend recorded that it was 'the most impressive meeting I have ever been to', and that:

> Tonight one felt that even in the awful present, where the forces of the past and of the future overlap and both so much that the present itself seems to have no claim to a place, the dark and negative power had been banished already. I felt happy to have had the chance of being for where I could feel in the centre of the conflict instead of hovering coldly at the circumference, with so much less hope.[33]

Other fundraising events arranged by the AIA included a dance and cabaret performance at the Seymour Hall in London in March 1938, with songs arranged by W.H. Auden and Benjamin Britten that were sung by Heidi Anderson. The event also featured dancing by Margot Fontaine and Robert Helpman, and a male striptease artist who according to Nan Youngman was 'really very funny, with marvellous arched looks while he took his braces off. He was quite a well-known comedian. It was really a dance and every once in a while there were these songs and acts'.[34] Britten was also to compose the incidental music for the documentary film Advance Democracy (1938), made by Ralph Bond in association with Basil Wright with words by Randall Swingler (the literary

Portraits

are being painted by a group of prominent artists including JACOB EPSTEIN, MARK GERTLER, ETHEL WALKER, CLARE LEIGHTON, ERIC GILL, ERIC RAVILIOUS, *etc., in conjunction with the* ARTISTS INTERNATIONAL ASSOCIATION. *All fees are given specially to*

Help Spanish Medical Aid

Portraits in oils from 5 to 500 guineas. Drawings from 1 guinea to 50 guineas.

Also caricatures, watercolours, pastels, sculptures, lithos, etchings, woodcuts, photographs.

Particulars from Secretary: Constance Biron, 20, Fitzroy Street, W.1.

ALL FEES DIRECTLY FOR SPAIN.

FIG. 50
Flier for the Artists International Association Portraits for Spain Scheme, 1938, 21.7 x 13.9cm, Private collection.

editor of the *Daily Worker)*, and the choral work *Ballad of Heroes*, to words by Swingler and Auden for a commemorative concert in 1939 to honour the fallen British members of the International Brigades. In July 1938 Britten's one-act verse play *Old Spain*, with a libretto by the poet and dramatist Montagu Slater, was performed by the Binyon Puppets at the Mercury Theatre in London, run by Helen Binyon and her sisters Margaret Binyon and Nicolete Gray.

In 1938 Ewan Phillips organised the AIA Portraits for Spain Scheme, through which artists would accept portrait commissions for an agreed fee that would be given to support the costs of sending the 'Artists Ambulance' to Spain.[35] Over 100 artists are listed on the prospectus for the scheme, offering work ranging from oils for between five to five hundred guineas (for an Augustus John portrait which was bought by the Cadbury Family)[36] to more modestly priced drawings (between 1 and 50 guineas), pastels, watercolours, lithographs, sculptures and even a photograph for 25 shillings by Helen Muspratt of the Cambridge photography partnership Ramsey and Muspratt that had taken the portrait of John Cornford known

FIG. 51
ERIC RAVILIOUS (1903–42)
Buscot 1939
Watercolour on paper
42 x 51.4 cm
Faringdon Collection Trust

as 'The Islanders' (fig. 37),. Participating artists included Peggy Angus, Michael Ayrton, Graham Bell, Quentin Bell, James Boswell, William Coldstream, Jacob Epstein, Mark Gertler, Eric Gill, Duncan Grant, Viscount Hastings, Clare Leighton, Otway McCannell, Robert Medley, Bernard Meninsky, Henry Moore, Peter Peri and Betty Rea amongst many others. The scheme raised enough funds to send a fully equipped field ambulance out to Spain. An article in the *Manchester Guardian* stated:

> Artists who have a hard enough time themselves in these days are generously giving their talents and time to help the supply of medical equipment to the British artists' ambulance in Spain by offering to make portraits in painting, sculpture or drawing for any client, the money going to the fund. Besides personal sitters, the artists are ready to undertake portraits of pets, houses, or even a chosen animal at the Zoo. Tokens, on the lines of book tokens, will be available, and it is hoped people may be induced to give a portrait token as a Christmas present.[37]

Those offering to paint a house included Edward Bawden, Graham Bell, Stephen Bone and Eric Ravilious, who accepted a commission from Lord Faringdon to paint a watercolour of his home at Buscot Park in Oxfordshire for 10 guineas (see fig. 51). Buscot was home to a temporary 'colony' for Basque refugee children in Hackford Lodge (now Basque House), and home to six exiled Spanish writers including Luis Cernuda, Arturo Barea and Pedro Garfias – who wrote the poem *Primavera en Eaton Hastings* (Spring in Eaton Hastings) inspired by his walks around Buscot Park. Lord Faringdon also sent his Rolls-Royce to be converted into an ambulance, which was driven out to Spain in January 1938 (fig. 52), and commissioned a portrait of his sister by Mark Gertler.[38]

Although the International Brigades were disbanded and 305 veterans arrived back in England in December 1938, the AIA continued its work to raise funds for Spanish relief, particularly for the thousands of refugees from Spain following the victory of the Nationalists. In January 1939 Graham Bell organised fellow realist artists from the Euston

Road School – including Rodrigo Moynihan, Lawrence Gowing, Victor Pasmore, Geoffrey Tibble, in addition to Carel Weight and probably Duncan Grant – to paint a series of banners based on Goya's *Disasters of War* that could be taken on demonstrations. As Coldstream and Gowing recalled:

> they were all 6′x 4′ on banner cloth, which we bought from a banner cloth shop in Whitechapel, which the Communist painters knew all about. Victor's one was of the bird picking out the entrails of an animal ... Graham Bell did a large number, and an associated little sketch of a man holding his nose with the smell of decomposing corpses. They were all lettered on the back with the inscription 'Hitler, Mussolini, Daladier, Chamberlain did this to Spain'.[39]

In a letter to his mother Bell described their effect on one viewer: 'we had them hanging on the wall in the art school and the model posing had to look more or less at one of them. After half an hour she burst into tears and was inconsolable.'[40] Although they were later seized during the Second World War by the Essex Home Guard, they were used at an 'Arms for Spain' rally in Trafalgar Square on 12 February 1939, and were exhibited as 'a broken frieze' that 'punctuated' the AIA's *Unity of Artists for Peace, Democracy and Cultural Development* exhibition at the Whitechapel Art Gallery in February and March 1939. The exhibition was visited by 40,000 visitors and opened by a random man called in off the street. Yet as Geoffrey Tibble was to comment about the banners: 'I may be a pessimist but it seems a bit late in the day to hope to alter things in Spain now. What a tragedy.'[41]

On 27 February Chamberlain and Daladier's governments recognised the Franco regime, and on 1 April 1939 victory was proclaimed after the last of the Republican forces surrendered. Although they had not been able to change the ultimate outcome of the war, the impassioned commitment of the 600 members of the AIA to the cause of Spain was nothing short of remarkable, and undoubtedly made a significant impact in raising funds for medical aid, support for humanitarian campaigns for refugees and victims of war, and in raising awareness through their art of the importance of defending democracy.

FIG. 52
Lord Faringdon's Rolls-Royce private car converted into an ambulance. Spain, January 1938. Photograph, The International Brigade Archive at the Marx Memorial Library (Box 33: Book 6)

1. Trevelyan 1957, p.57 and p.72.
2. Morris 1983, p.34.
3. *Daily Express* cutting in Marx Memorial Library, IBMA, Box A-12, file Bro.
4. Brinkman , typewritten account written in Barcelona on 30 August 1936 (MML, IBMA, Box 21/B/1a), quoted in Tom Buchanan, *The Impact of the Spanish Civil War on Britain: War, Loss and Memory* (Brighton: Sussex Academic Press, 2007), p.79. There are conflicting accounts of how she died, but Buchanan accepts that the Brinkman account seems most likely.
5. The catalogue for the Felicia Browne exhibition featured a foreword by Duncan Grant who, like many others, was unfamiliar with Browne's work before her unfortunate death. Grant wrote of being 'exceedingly glad of the opportunity' to see her drawings, 'I have never seen any of her work before, therefore I was unable to consider her drawings in relation to her sculpture. I do not think I should have ever thought if them as a sculptor's drawings had you not told me. They are so alive, but they exist on their own merit, and do not suggest studies for another purpose. Even the slightest express such a tense awareness of character, be it in houses, men or beasts, that they are never incomplete, something deeply felt is expressed in a way that is quickly comprehended'.
6. It seems likely that the character of Joyce Emily in the 1961 novel *The Prime of Miss Jean Brodie* by Muriel Spark was based on Browne. In the novel Miss Brody encourages Joyce to enlist to fight in Spain (for Franco), but she is killed before she sees action.
7. It seems Browne's main motivation for working in the tea shop was not the meagre wages but trying to get the staff politically aware and unionised.
8. Morris, *ibid*, p.31.
9. Spender quoted in Boyd Haycock 2012, p.145.
10. Thomas 1977, p.348.
11. This is recounted in Spender 1991.
12. Ravilious, quoted in Alan Powers, *Imagined Realities* (London: Imperial War Museum, 2003), p.64.
13. Coldstream to Rake, 18 January 1937. Tate Gallery, Coldstream papers, TGA 8922.4.548.
14. Vanessa Bell letter to Julian Bell, Saturday 10 October 1936, VII-27, in Marler 1993, pp 422–6.
15. These posters are untraced, but some loose sketches by Grant and Angelica Garnett are in the Angelica Garnett Gift at Charleston – I am grateful to Dr Darren Clarke for bringing these to my attention. See Spalding 1984.
16. Vanessa Bell, quoted in Spalding, *ibid*, p.292.
17. Vanessa Bell, letter to Julian Bell, Sunday 22 November 1936, VII-29 in Marler, *op.cit.*, pp 427–30.
18. Thomas, *ibid*, page 590 n.2.
19. Julian Bell, *We Did Not Fight 1914–18: Experiences of War Resisters* (London: Cobden Sanderson, 1935).
20. It was subsequently acquired by Lord Faringdon, the socialist peer who had created a refuge for Basque refugees at his home Buscot Park.
21. Reg Turner in Morris, *ibid*, p.34.
22. It is likely that they are either reading *Spain in Revolt* by Harry Gannes and Theodore Repard or Arthur Koestler's *Spanish Testament*.
23. One of the newspaper boards refers to events in Spain, the other to HMS *Thetis*, a British submarine which sank in the Mediterranean on 1 June 1939 with the loss of 99 lives – resulting in an attempt by one of the widows to bring a claim of negligence against the shipbuilders, which was blocked by the Admirality claiming Crown Priviledge.
24. *The Times*, 18 June 1937.
25. Trevelyan, *ibid*, p.78.
26. T.S. Eliot, pp 56–7 (see Morris, 1983, pp.56–7)
27. Blunt, *The Spectator,* 10 June 1938.
28. See Spalding, *op. cit.*, p.294. At the Albert Hall Concert Vanessa Bell donated 10 shillings, and Virginia and Leonard Woolf gave a pound each. See Spalding *op. cit.*, p.296.
29. 'Spain's Struggle for Freedom: A Notable Manifesto' in Letters to the Editor, *Manchester Guardian*, 19 June 1937 – signed by Paul Langevin, Matisse, Picasso, Lascelles Abercrombie, Vanessa Bell, Havelock Ellis, Duncan Grant, Le Gros Clark, John MacMurray, Sybil Thorndike and Virginia Woolf.
30. William Townsend, 24 June 1937, Forge 1976, p.40.
31. The drawing titled *Weeping Woman* was subsequently acquired by Roland Penrose, and was accepted by H.M. Government in lieu of tax and allocated to the Tate Gallery in 1995.
32. 'Spanish Relief Efforts: Albert Hall Meeting £1,000 Collected for Children', *Manchester Guardian*, 25 June 1937.
33. William Townsend, 24 June 1937, *op. cit.*, pp 40–1.
34. Nan Youngman quoted in Morris, *ibid*, p.33.
35. Ewan Phillips, one of the founder members of the AIA, had been one of the first students at the Courtauld Institute under Anthony Blunt. He was a founder of the Artists Refugee Committee and after serving in the Monuments, Fine Art and Archives Unit in the Second World War became the first Director of the Institute of Contemporary Arts.
36. George W. Cadbury wrote to Ewan Phillips in January 1939, before his father had sat to Augustus John: 'As the need for Spanish relief is so urgent I enclose a cheque for £500 now and will take steps at a later date to recover it from the Board of Directors.' See Buchanan, *ibid*, p.91 and uncatalogued Ewan Phillips papers in Tate Gallery Archive.
37. 'Portraits for Spain' in 'Our London Correspondence', *Manchester Guardian*, 16 December 1937.
38. Photograph of Max Colin (Cohen) departing in Lord Faringdon's Rolls-Royce (see fig. 52), January 1938. Marx Memorial Library, International Brigade Archives, Box 33: Book 6/14 a.
39. Coldstream and Gowing, quoted in Morris, *ibid*, p.54.
40. Tate Gallery, Graham Bell papers TGA 947.3, c.13 March 1939.
41. Geoffrey Tibble to William Townsend. UCL, Townsend Papers. Letters 1926–46, 30 January 1939.

3 LONELY VOLCANOES: British Artistic Support for the Nationalists

FIG. 53
WYNDHAM LEWIS
(1882–1957)
The Surrender of Barcelona
1934–7
Oil on canvas
83.8 x 59.7 cm
Tate, purchased 1947

Whilst the majority of avant-garde British artists, writers and intellectuals in the 1930s were supportive of Republican Spain, it is harder to quantify those whose support was broadly for the Nationalists, or at least not for the Republicans. 'There's Wyndham Lewis fuming out of sight, that lonely old volcano of the Right', wrote W.H. Auden of the former Vorticist artist in his 1937 *Letter to Lord Byron*.[1] Yet Lewis was by no means a lone voice, nor of a completely politically fixed position. Indeed, in the same year Lewis described himself as being 'the most broadminded "leftwinger" in England'.[2] During the decade of the 1930s Lewis moved from publishing his uncritical book *Hitler* in 1931, in which he declared that the Führer was 'a Man of Peace', to *The Hitler Cult* in 1939 in which he denounced Nazism.

Whilst usually clear about identifying themselves as against communism, some of the artists and writers that nominally supported Franco also sought to distance themselves from fascism – being mindful of the wider association between the Nationalists and fascism in Germany and Italy.

When asked by Nancy Cunard which side he was on for her celebrated survey 'Authors Take Sides on the Spanish War' in 1937, the novelist Evelyn Waugh declared: 'If I were a Spaniard I should be fighting for General Franco. As an Englishman I am not in the predicament of choosing between two evils. I am not a Fascist nor shall I become one unless it were the only alternative to Marxism. It is mischievous to suggest that such a choice is imminent.'[3]

Apart from Wyndham Lewis, who could be described as a modernist of the right, the supporters of the Nationalists were often both artistically and politically conservative – suspicious not only of avant-garde art, but also concerned by the spread of communism from Russia and by reports of anti-Catholic violence and the destruction of historic artworks and churches by left-wing anarchists. Commenting on this position, George Orwell was to observe in 1938 in a review of *The Church in Spain* by pro-Franco writer E. Allison Peers: 'all church-burning, priest-shooting and anticlerical violence generally are supposed to have their roots in Communism and its Spanish variant, Anarchism, which is inseparable from "hatred of God". It is not, Professor Peers thinks, a question of hostility to a corrupt church, but of "a cold, calculated, determined attempt to destroy institutional religion throughout the country".[4]

In the 1938 Royal Academy exhibition Sir William Russell Flint exhibited *In their Own Homes*. Subtitled *Spain's Agony of Civil War 1936–38* (current location unknown) it amounted to a direct statement in support of the Nationalists. Flint had travelled extensively in the Iberian Peninsula in the 1920s and 1930s, painting views of 'Old Spain' with Mediterranean townscapes, bullfighters and nubile flamenco dancers. *In their Own Homes* employed similar subject matter, but with a shocking twist – a group of such women being lined up and shot by Republican riflemen.[5] 'Cheerfully rich in colour, its theme is a little horrific…', observed critic F.C. Tilney in his conservative art magazine *Art and Reason*: 'The theme is tragic enough, and must bring home to visitors Spain's agony.'[6] Such artworks were often motivated as much by concern for the suffering of humanity as those created by supporters of the Republic, and served to expose the uneasy and inconvenient political narrative of Republican atrocities that many of their supporters chose to overlook, or put down to Nationalist propaganda. As novelist Eleanor Smith wrote in response to Cunard's survey: 'Naturally, I am a warm adherent of General Franco's, being like all of us, a humanitarian. The destruction of so many beautiful objects, and the massacre of so many innocent persons, makes one pity profoundly the ignorant red masses – subsidised by Russia – in Spain. Do you not agree?'[7] Similar ideas were the basis of a satirical painting with the ironic title *'The Reds are Really Not Bad Sorts, or the Tastes of War'* (fig. 54) by Sir Francis Rose, who had been part of Gertrude Stein's circle in Paris in the 1920s. The 'Reds' of the title are depicted waving a communist flag and holding a severed head in a bomb-damaged street littered with a broken crucifix (referencing the anti-clerical attacks) and a bloody corpse, with crystal chandeliers hung from trees (to make a point about the looting and distribution of wealth). One part of a quasi-religious dual-head in the sky cries tears of blood – perhaps a symbol of Spain wrought apart.

Rose wrote without irony in his autobiography that 'the star of Spain was the honest, hardworking General Franco, who had inherited the burden of leading the loyalists.'[8] He bemoaned the 'sentimental intellectuals' that supported the Republicans, complaining that all his friends had been enemies of Franco and that personally he had:

hoped and felt certain that Franco would win. It is impossible to describe the hate one feels during a civil war: the loathing I had for the International Brigade formed by intellectuals who were really acting as left-wing spies for foreign powers, beachcomers, layabouts, and old prison hands seeking any employment. The heroic defence of the Alcazar at Toledo made one proud, just as one was disgusted by the ignorant brutality of the International Brigade.[9]

Rose's wholehearted and enthusiastic support for the Nationalists was a rare position, particularly as he was writing after the events of the Second World War. His take on the 'unfortunate' bombing of Guernica was chillingly flippant – it had 'inspired Picasso to paint a great picture that was more important to the world than the destruction of a slum near Bilbao'.[10] Later in his autobiography he was to state that,

the fall of Madrid and Barcelona were the most joyful days of my life, as it was a real victory Franco had won … Only in Spain could peace exist, and Franco's legitimate triumph was more than the 1945 conquest by a group of allies of a group of foreign enemies. I could hear the words of Röhm crying out when Franco's army won. A soldier must be a pacifist, the enemy of warmongers, the maintainer of the race, and the father of the people. Franco has been this for many years in a purely Christian way.[11]

The experiences of those artists and writers who had been in Spain around the start of the conflict often determined their subsequent position, particularly if they witnessed the anti-clerical violence. Over 4,184 secular priests, 2,365 monks and 283 nuns were killed in the Spanish Civil War,

FIG. 54
FRANCIS ROSE (1909–79)
The Reds are Really Not Bad Sorts, or the Tastes of War
September 1936
Gouache on paper
Courtesy of Jane England, England & Co.

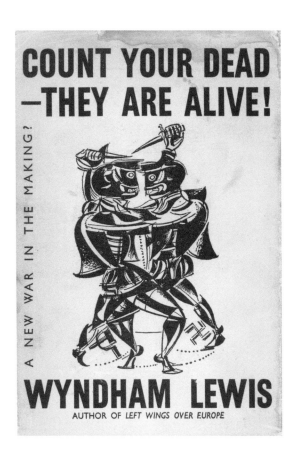

mostly in the first weeks. The poet Edith Sitwell had been staying in Catalonia in the summer of 1936, but left around 15 July due to the outbreak of the war. Her former governess Helen Rootham and friend Evelyn Weil remained and hid a priest in their home, who was dragged out and narrowly avoided being shot. As Sitwell wrote to the Russian artist Pavel Tchelitchew of the incident: 'You who know the horrors of revolution will understand all this,'[12] and thereafter she wanted nothing to do with the war.

Sitwell's friend the poet Roy Campbell was similarly shocked by the church burnings and attacks on nuns and priests. A Catholic convert, he and his wife sheltered several Carmelite monks in their home in Toledo where they had lived since 1935. He was severely beaten and paraded through the streets by government 'Red' guards for his widely known political and religious beliefs. Many of the monks were subsequently shot in the street and he later immortalised them in the poem *The Carmelites of Toledo* (1937). On returning to England after being evacuated with other British subjects on the HMS *Maine* in August 1936, Campbell was deeply offended by the pro-Republican sympathies in Britain and became avowedly anti-Marxist. At the suggestion of Wyndham Lewis he met Sir

Oswald Mosley in 1936, and his poetry featured in Mosley's *British Union Quarterly* (although he declined to become the official poet of the British fascist movement). Campbell returned to Spain as a correspondent for Catholic newspaper the *Tablet* in June 1937. After a period in Italy in 1938 he returned to Spain in April 1939, travelling to Madrid to witness the victory parade of Franco's forces. He subsequently wrote the epic poem *Flowering Rifle*, which condemned the British intelligentsia for its 'ruling passion' of 'humanitarianism', which 'sides automatically with the Dog against the Man, the Jew against the Christian, the black against the white, the servant against the master, the criminal against the judge'.[13] The poem caused widespread consternation amongst the Left, leading Stephen Spender to describe it as 'a kind of three-decker sandwich consisting of one layer of invective against the intellectuals of the Left, the International Brigade, the Spanish Republican Army, etc; a second layer of autobiography concerning the exploits of Mr Campbell and his flowering rifle; and a top layer of rhapsody about Franco and his colleagues, who are treated as nothing less than angels'.[14]

Amidst debates about whether Spain's artistic heritage was being valued and cared for by either

FIG. 55
WYNDHAM LEWIS
(1882–1957)
*Count Your Dead -
They are Alive!* 1937
Bookjacket
Estate of Mrs G. A.
Wyndham Lewis by
permission of the Wyndham
Lewis Memorial Trust

FIG. 56
EDWARD BURRA (1905–76)
The Torturers c. 1935
Pencil, watercolour
and gouache
76 x 56 cm
Private Collection

side, and presentations in London of Spanish Old Masters by artists including Goya and El Greco (see chapter 1), Wyndham Lewis' comment on the contemporary situation was to reinterpret the visual language of historic artworks. In around 1937 he painted two 'realist fantasies' drawing on accounts of Spanish history by nineteenth-century American historian William H. Prescott: *The Armada* (1937, Vancouver Art Gallery, Canada) and *The Surrender of Barcelona* (fig. 53).[15] Both present modernist interpretations of historical events in an over-layering of past and present. In the case of the latter picture Lewis recalled: 'I set out to paint as Fourteenth Century [sic] scene as I should do it could I be transported there, without too great a change in the time adjustment involved.'[16] In fact, it was a fifteenth-century scene based on the surrender of Barcelona after the siege of 1472 and subsequent victorious entry of Ferdinand of Aragon and his wife Isabella of Castile (whose marriage represented the unification of Spain). Prescott had concluded, 'thus ended this long, disastrous Civil War'.[17] The helmeted soldiers amassed before Lewis' post-Cubist interpretation of a Renaissance cityscape reflect his description of frontier guards as cloaked figures that 'had become portentous medieval silhouettes'.[18] Men on horseback accompanied by lancers enter the city – an allusion to the composition of Diego Velásquez' *The Surrender of Breda* (1635, Museo del Prado, Madrid), but without the chivalrous gesture at its heart. Although Lewis did not attempt a literal depiction of the emaciated figures suffering from famine that were described by Prescott, the hanged man at the centre of the composition serves to convey a sense of suffering and the meting out of justice, or indeed injustice, by the dominant power. In the window of a tower above this figure is the artist at his easel, possibly a comment on the role of the artist in relation to politics. As Alan Munton has commented: 'the armoured men in the painting portend no good for the artist in his tower, which is so far from being an ivory tower that it gives him a unique vantage-point from which to observe the violent, arrogant, casual, but power laden occupation that is being organised around him.'[19]

Wyndham Lewis had felt it was against Britain's interests to support the Republicans in the Civil War and was as critical of communist activity in Spain as Campbell, although not perhaps for such personal religious reasons. In 1934–5 he had written the satirical and political novel *The Revenge for Love*, published in May 1937. It begins and ends in Spain, revolving around the characters Percy Hardcastle (a British communist organiser based on Lewis' acquaintance, the English novelist Ralph Bates – a communist who was active in Spain before the war and who was to become a key figure in the International Brigades) and an impoverished painter called Victor Stamp and his lover Margot Savage, who become involved in a scheme to smuggle guns across the Franco-Spanish border.

These themes were developed in his pro-appeasement books *Left Wings Over Europe: Or, How to Make a War about Nothing* (1936) and *Count Your Dead: They are Alive! Or, a New War in the Making* (1937), in which Franco is presented as 'an ordinary old fashioned anti-monarchical Spanish *liberal*' who is defending Spain against Russian communism. Lewis felt that Britain was anti-German in its response to the civil war and too sympathetic to the Russians. The cover image of *Count Your Dead* (fig. 55) features two dagger-wielding stylised warriors in an ideological battle – one has a Nazi swastika by his side and the other a communist hammer and sickle. It relates to his paintings from around this time, including *Red and Black Principle* (1936, Santa Barbara Museum of Art, USA), a painting whose title and imagery of two military figures, one bearing the fasces, suggest a communist/fascist dichotomy that could even be interpreted as a form of balance of powers. Lewis' own recognition of the suffering of the victims of war and polarisation of politics was to change during the later 1930s, particularly after visiting Berlin and Warsaw which led him to change his views regarding Nazism (in 1939 Lewis published the philosemitic *The Jews: Are they Human?*, a defence of the Jews, and *The Hitler Cult* which attacked Nazism). Following the occupation of Barcelona by the Nationalists on 26 January 1939, which led to a massacre, Lewis changed the title of the picture from *The Siege of Barcelona* to *The Surrender of Barcelona*. That

FIG. 58
EDWARD BURRA (1905–76)
Medusa 1938
Watercolour, pencil and
gouache on paper
115 x 112 cm
Manchester Art Gallery

Lewis had donated a picture to an auction in aid of Republican Spain in 1938 also suggests that despite his anti-communist position he had shifted some ground as the war continued. In 1939 he wrote of the 'Catalan sun' setting 'in human blood, alas! As Barcelona falls, and the phalangist standard is unfurled there, we can see that is the end of a chapter – of painting, among other things'.[20]

There are striking parallels in the work and experiences of Edward Burra to Wyndham Lewis and other British supporters of the Nationalists, and yet it would not be accurate to clearly identify Burra as a committed supporter of *either* side in the conflict. He was hugely fond of Spain, its art and literature, and told John Rothenstein that he was 'haunted by Spain, and obsessed by Spanish civilisation'.[21] He had painted a series of '*Duennas*' inspired by the elderly Spanish governesses in Miguel de Cervantes' *Don Quixote* in the early 1930s, and trips to the country in 1933, 1935 and from April to July 1936 were to result in numerous paintings on Spanish themes featuring at first flamenco dancers and bull fights, but subsequently much darker themes. As his friend Clover de Pertinez was to observe: 'the Spanish Civil War and increasing ill-health revealed the tragic sense of life in Ed that had long been latent in him. He sensed the Civil War in the air a year before it broke out in the summer of 1936.'[22] As early as 1935 Burra had begun to paint images that touched on the violence and sense of social unease in Spain in works such as *The Torturers* (fig. 56), which features a group of naked red male figures, one of whom wears the kind of hat worn by a *matador de toros* (bullfighter). There is no actual violence depicted in the scene, only the potential for violence set within a dark back alley away from the sun-lit main promenade – a metaphor for the simmering tensions beneath Spanish society. Burra was highly conscious of the work of Spanish Old Masters he had seen in the Prado, such as El Greco, Diego Velásquez, Franciso de Zurbarán, and particularly Goya, and of the frescoes of monks being tortured by Juan Sánchez Cotán in Granada.[23] These artists' work was to inform his own increasingly Mannerist elongated figures in historic settings.

Burra had been shocked to witness the church burnings, and later related to John Rothenstein how:

Just before the beginning of the Spanish Civil War I happened to be in Madrid. One day when I was lunching with some Spanish friends … smoke kept blowing by the restaurant window. I asked where it came from. 'Oh it's nothing', someone answered with a shake of impatience, 'it's only a church being burnt!' That made me feel sick. It was terrifying: constant strikes, churches on fire and pent up hatred everywhere. Everybody knew that something appalling was about to happen.[24]

Between 1936 and 1939 Burra painted a series of ambiguous haunting images peopled by torturers, duennas, the Fates, skeletal hangmen and other hooded figures. Although the violence in Burra's work is usually understated, it spills over in *Beelzebub* (fig. 59) in which a marauding throng with bloody weapons clashes violently in the ruins of a church, whose columns and walls lie at the feet of a powerful

FIG. 59
EDWARD BURRA (1905–76)
Beelzebub 1937–38
Watercolour on paper
154.9 x 111.8 cm
Courtesy Lefevre Fine Art

FIG. 60
EDWARD BURRA (1905–76)
War in the Sun 1938
Watercolour on paper
156 × 112 cm
Private Collection

and devilish red being that leers out at the viewer as if egging the violence on. The composition with the elongated figure of Beezlzebub facing into the scene at the right is taken in part from El Greco's *Laocoön* (1610–14), whilst the interior recalls the arched spaces of El Greco's *Christ Driving the Money Changers from the Temple* (1600). Similarly, in *Medusa* (fig. 58) a malign mythical figure presides over a horrific scene of death and destruction – a mound of semi-naked corpses that have been hanged hangs over one shoulder of her scaly body.[25] In Greek mythology looking directly into the eyes of Medusa (who stares directly out of the image at the viewer) would turn onlookers to stone. Neither work explicitly addressed the conflict in Spain, but it is there in the atmosphere. As Andrew Causey was to note: 'it was Spain above all that set the conditions for his art in this period, and fixed his interests in war, violence and destruction, and the drama and ritual of Catholicism.'[26]

In *The Watcher* (fig. 57) a menacing stand-off takes place between a dark figure cloaked in red and another wearing a kind of red *galero* (cardinal's hat), and bearing an elaborately aggressive barbed lance.

It is unclear which figure is on the defensive, and which is aggressive. As with *Medusa* the moment of confrontation is set amid the ruins of a past civilisation, but the background figure lying prone over a cauldron adds to the unnerving sense of suffering that adds to the immediacy of the scene. The connection between past and present is more explicit in *War in the Sun* (fig. 60), in which a modern tank, artillery gun and armoured vehicles appear in the theatrical setting of pockmarked Renaissance buildings. The soldiers do not wear military uniforms, but instead the brightly coloured heraldic robes of medieval knights. There is an affinity to Wyndham Lewis' *Surrender of Barcelona*; indeed Lewis wrote of Burra's work: 'I share Burra's emotions regarding war; when I see the purple bottoms of his military ruffians in athletic action against other stout though fiendish fellows, I recognise a brother.'[27]

Rothenstein was apparently shocked when Burra admitted that he was pro-Franco but told him not to mention it when being interviewed for his *Modern Painters* book.[28] Burra had been loosely affiliated to the British Surrealist group,

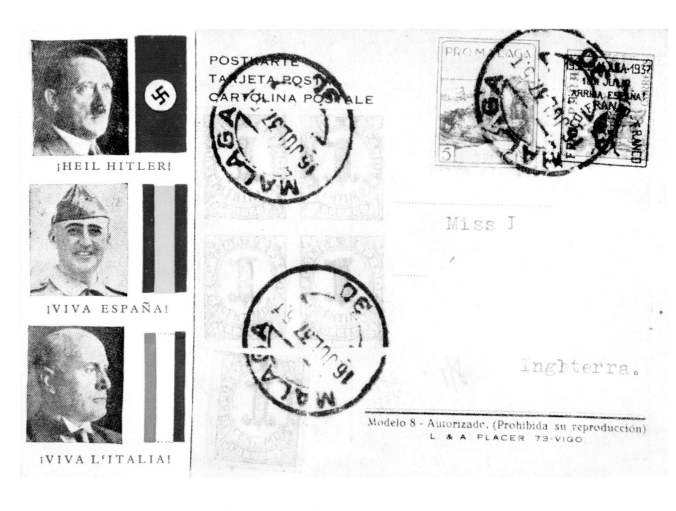

which was pro-Republican, as were many of his friends including John Banting, Paul Nash, Barbara Ker-Seymer (who become romantically involved with Republican supporter Wogan Phillips), and Clover Pritchard, who married the Republican Antonio Pertinez. Attempting to rationalise Burra's position, Rothenstein expressed his doubts:

> whether in fact he had Fascist sympathies and believed he was prejudiced against their opponents by the burning of churches he saw. I never heard him express such sympathies – being pro-Franco apart – which I believe I would have done had he nourished them. One of his many peculiarities was that he was well informed on many subjects, politics (though they did not greatly interest him) included.[29]

Burra was evidently opposed to fascism in other ways, and in addition to participating in Surrealist exhibitions he had been included in exhibitions of the anti-fascist AIA such as The Social Scene in 1934. Like Evelyn Waugh's response to Nancy Cunard it could be, as Jane Stevenson suggests, that Burra 'was pro-Franco without being Fascist at all, and asked Rothenstein not to talk about it because he did not think such as position was comprehensible'.[30] Throughout his life Burra was ostensibly apolitical, believing in people as individuals and never explicitly expressing public support for fascism, communism or any other political unit. His paintings in response to the Spanish Civil War are some of the most powerful images to emerge from the conflict, but that power comes largely from their political ambiguity, and the theme of tragedy upon a more exalted level. As Vita Sackville West was to respond to Cunard:

> I dislike Communism and Fascism equally; and, in fact, cannot see any difference between them, except in their names. It seems to me that each bully and oppress the individual; and, through the individual, Society at large. That is why I cannot make up my mind to take either side in the Spanish quarrel, which is really a quarrel between Communism and Fascism in Europe, not only in Spain.[31]

1. W.H. Auden and Louis MacNeice, *Letters from Iceland* (London: Faber, 1937).
2. Wyndham Lewis, *Blasting and Bombardiering* (London: Eyre and Spottiswoode, *1937*).
3. Cunard 1937, unpaginated.
4. George Orwell, 'Review of *The Church in Spain 1737–1937* by E. Allison Peers', *New English Weekly*, 24 November 1938.
5. The painting was reproduced in *Royal Academy Illustrated* (London: Royal Academy, 1938); its current whereabouts is unknown.
6. F.C. Tilney, *Art and Reason*, vol.IV, no.41, May 1938.
7. Cunard, *ibid*, unpaginated.
8. Francis Rose, *Saying Life: The Memoirs of Sir Francis Rose* (London: Cassell, 1961), p.276.
9. Rose, *ibid*, p.353.
10. Rose, *ibid*, p276
11. Rose, *ibid*, p.379.
12. Greene, Edith Sitwell: Avant Garde Poet, English Genius (London: Virago, 2012)
13. Roy Campbell, *Flowering Rifle* (London, Green & Co., 1939).
14. Stephen Spender, 'The Talking Bronco: A Review of Roy Campbell, *Flowering Rifle*, 1939', Cunningham 1980, p.441.
15. William H. Prescott, *History of the Reign of Ferdinand and Isabella the Catholic* (n.d.), ed. John Foster Kirk (London: Swan Sonnenschein, 1841).
16. Wyndham Lewis, *Rude Assignment* (London, Hutchinson & Co., 1951), p.140.
17. Prescott, *ibid*.
18. Lewis 1952, p.290.
19. Alan Munton, 'Wyndham Lewis and Spain: Anarchism, Cliché Image', *Wyndham Lewis* (Madrid: Fundación Juan March, 2010), p.84.
20. Wyndham Lewis, *The Hitler Cult* (London: Dent, 1939), p.18.
21. Rothenstein, John, *Edward Burra* (Harmondsworth: Penguin, 1945), p.31.
22. Clover de Pertinez, in William Chappell (ed.), *Edward Burra: A Painter Remembered by His Friends* (London: Andre Deutsch, 1982), p.80.
23. John Rothenstein recorded that when he visited Burra's studio in September 1942 'the walls were covered almost entirely by photographs of paintings, many by Spanish masters, including El Greco, Zurbaran, Goya as well as Signorelli, Tiepolo, Magnaso, among them pictures clipped from newspapers and periodicals, many representing dramatic incidents'. In 'Edward Burra as an Artist', Chappell, *ibid*, p.45.
24. Rothenstein in Chapel, *ibid*.
25. There are also significant similarities between this work and Wyndham Lewis' *Inferno* (1937, National Gallery of Victoria, Melbourne, Australia), which features a hellish vision of bodies piled up in the foreground.
26. Causey, in Arts Council 1985, p.45.
27. Wyndham Lewis, 'The London Galleries', *Listener*, 9 June 1949.
28. Chappell, *ibid*, p.46.
29. Chappell, *ibid*, p.46.
30. Stevenson 2007, p.207.
31. Cunard, *ibid*.

AIXAFEM EL FEIXISME

Editat per la Comissaria de Propaganda de la Generalitat de Catalunya.   (Fot. Català)

4 HELP SPAIN!
Poster Design and the
Spanish Aid Movements

All the posters on the walls
All the leaflets in the streets
Are mutilated, destroyed or run in rain
Their words blotted out with tears
Skin peeling from their bodies
In the victorious hurricane

Stephen Spender, *Fall of a City*

FIG. 62
PERE CATALÀ PIC
(1889–1971)
Aixafem el Feixisme
(Let's Squash Fascism) 1936
Lithograph on paper
104.6 x 75.5 cm
Manuel Moreno

During the first year of the Second World War the Surrealist artist John Banting wrote an article in *Horizon* magazine in which he compared what he felt was the poor standard of current propaganda posters to the superior examples created by the Spanish Republican government during the Civil War. He bemoaned the fact that nearly a year into the later war 'we have produced no remarkable posters and the sociological and political level of which we have remains much the same as that of nearly twenty-five years ago'.[1] He had offered to take examples of the Spanish posters to show the Ministry of Information, but was turned down, perhaps because of the association with Soviet revolutionary poster art. Banting's comments in his 'Notes on Posters of the Spanish Republican Government' had been timed to coincide with an exhibition at Marx House in London presenting the posters that he had collected during his trip to Spain from October to December 1937.[2] Looking back on his trip to Spain Banting recalled how, 'I had great difficulty in collecting these posters, which were issued not only by the Ministry of Propaganda but also by the offices of the numerous political parties and government services. However, *because of* rather than *in spite of* my being a foreigner special consideration was given to me'.[3]

Amongst the four posters illustrated in the article was one of the most striking pieces of propaganda to emerge from the Spanish Civil War: *¿QUE HACES TU PARA EVITAR ESTO? AYUDA A MADRID' (What are you doing to prevent this? Help Madrid)* (fig. 64). The poster was issued by the Ministerio de Propaganda and printed between 4 November 1936 and 17 May 1937 in three languages (English, French and Spanish), and also issued with the title 'Send food to Spain' for the National Joint Committee for Spanish Relief. This remarkable example of photomontage created a potent visual association between the suffering of innocent victims and the Nationalist's bombing of Spanish cities. It was widely used in Spanish aid events in Britain. The photographer Helen Muspratt, for example, recorded the poster in the incongruous home counties setting of a churchyard at Ringwood in Hampshire, where it formed the focus for an Aid Spain auction.[4]

Depictions of the vulnerable – the elderly, injured, women and children – appearing before scenes of aerial bombardment and devastation were a common motif in such posters, as in *HELP SPAIN* (fig. 2). The connection between the Civil War and the wider European fight against fascism was also succinctly conveyed in the 1936 poster *Aixafem el Feixisme* (*Let's Squash Fascism*) by Pere Català I Pic (fig. 62), in which a swastika is stamped on by a foot wearing the *alpargatas* (traditional peasant footwear), suggesting that the common people will crush the fascists. The Surrealist poet Mary Low mentioned seeing the poster, in the memoir she co-authored with fellow Surrealist poet Juan Brea, after an evening at the theatre in Barcelona in 1936: 'we stood outside the columned portico, in front of us a poster flapped in the rain: a foot in a Catalan sandal crushing a swastika with negligent, unquestioned strength.'[5] Such defiant gestures were less common in posters intended for an international audience, which tended to aim for a sympathetic response by highlighting the humanitarian crisis. Indeed, the photomontage of the woman and child

in fig. 64 was in fact cropped from a photo of a demonstration (fig.63) captioned 'See the widows carrying their children, These little ones will the revengers tomorrow'. Members of the crowd, including the child, hold up their fists defiantly in the anti-fascist salute, revealing that the tenor of the original photograph was changed considerably.

Perhaps the most arresting and iconic of any of the posters produced to encourage support for Republican Spain was one titled *Madrid: The 'Military' Practices of the Rebels* (fig. 65). Issued by the Ministerio de Propaganda, and believed to be by a designer known as 'Augusto', it featured a photomontage of a dead child marked with an identification tag before a sky filled with a fleet of bomber planes in formation. Underneath is the dark warning *'If you tolerate this your children will be next',*[6] aimed to challenge the position of non-intervention in France and Britain, where the poster was issued in their respective languages. The image was taken from one of many photographs issued by the Republican government of children killed in the bombing raids that were issued by the Republican

FIG. 63
ANONYMOUS
Photograph of a demonstration in Spain, c.1937 Published by the Ministerio de Propaganda, International Brigade Archive at the Marx Memorial Library

FIG. 64
ANONYMOUS
What are you doing to prevent this?
November 1936– May 1937
Half- tone, lithograph on paper
80 x 56 cm
Manuel Moreno

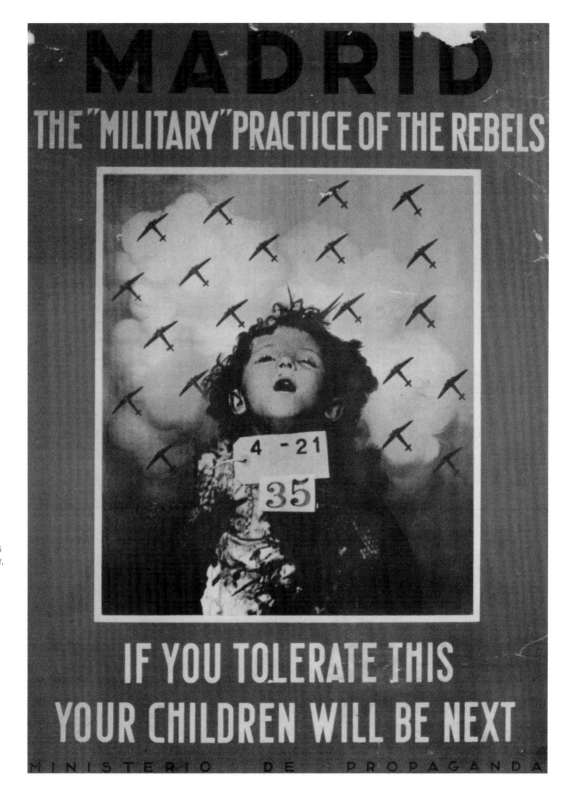

FIG. 65
UNKNOWN
Madrid: The Military Practices of the Rebels 1936
Off-set lithograph on paper, published by Ministerio de Propaganda
66.3 x 49.2 cm
Courtesy of the People's History Museum

FIG. 66
FRANK BRANGWYN
(1867–1956)
For the relief of Women and Children in Spain 1937
Lithograph on paper
Published by the General Relief Fund for Distressed Women and Children in Spain
155 x 105cm
Leicestershire County Council Artworks Collection

FIG. 67
Frank Brangwyn in his
Ditchling Studio, c.1937–8

government. Records in the Marx Memorial Library reveal that the photograph of the dead girl was taken on 31 October 1936, showing María Santiago Robert who had been killed in an aerial bombardment on Getafe the previous day.[7] The same image featured as the frontispiece to George Barker's poem *Elegy on Spain* (1939), which was 'dedicated to the photograph of a child killed in an air raid on Barcelona'.[8]

O ecstatic is this head of five-year joy –
Captured its butterfly rapture on a paper:
And not the rupture of the right eye may
Make any less this prettier than a picture.
O now, my minor moon, dead as meat
Slapped on a negative plate, I hold
The crime of the bloody time in my hand.

Light, light with that lunar death our fate;
Make more dazzling with your agony's gold
The death that lays us all in the sand.
Gaze with that gutted eye on our endeavour
To be the human brute, not the brute human:
And if I feel your gaze upon me ever,
I'll wear the robe of blood that love illumines.

The Republican government's Director General of Fine Art, Josep Renau, a practising artist who designed numerous propaganda posters including the photomontages that featured in the Spanish Pavilion at the Paris Worlds Fair in 1937, recognised poster design as an art, but believed that the artist's personal expression should be secondary to the legibility of the message being conveyed. In Renau's view, 'the poster maker, as an artist, knows a disciplined freedom, a freedom conditioned by objective demands, external to his individual will. Thus, for the poster artist the simple question of expressing his own sensibility and emotion is neither legitimate nor practically realisable, if not in the service of an objective goal.'[9]

It is not surprising that the most successful posters by British artists were by those with experience in commercial design. These posters were often rich in artistic and cultural references to the art of the past, which may have been lost on working-class viewers. The majority of British posters highlighted the humanitarian situation and aimed to raise funds for Spanish aid campaigns. A notable example was the poster designed by Sir Frank Brangwyn RA in 1937 entitled *Spain*, in support of the General Relief Fund for Distressed Women and Children in Spain (fig. 66). Unlike many of the artists who actively supported the Republican cause, Brangwyn was Roman Catholic. In this respect it is significant that the General Relief Fund was non-partisan and under the patronage of leaders from different faiths – the Church of Scotland, the Archbishop of Canterbury, Catholic clergy, the Free Churches and the Chief Rabbi – and it was 'concerned with the sick and wounded, and the women and children, on both sides of the Spanish Civil War'.[10] As a socially engaged pacifist Brangwyn had previously produced several posters for campaigns such as the Abolition of Capital Punishment and the French Benevolent Society, as well as supporting organisations such as the Red Cross.

Brangwyn's commitment and identification with the project is evidenced by the quantity of studies he created for the poster (fig. 68), and the fact that he chose to be photographed alongside the

FIG. 68
FRANK BRANGWYN
(1867–1956)
Four studies for the poster
For the Relief of Women and Children in Spain 1937
Chalk, ink, gouache and pencil on buff paper
Each approx. 25 x 17cm
On loan from Scarborough Museums Trust, SCAAG
462, 463, 465, 466

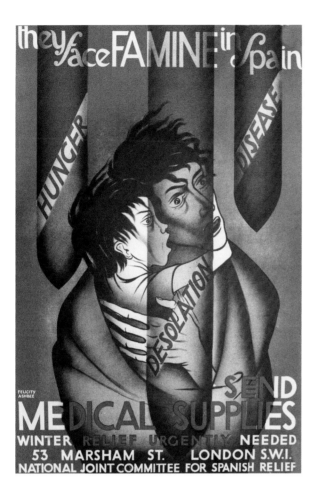

FIG. 69
FELICITY ASHBEE
(1867–1956)
*They Face Famine in Spain:
Send Medical Supplies* 1937
Off-set lithograph on paper,
published by the National
Joint Committee for
Spanish Relief
76.3 x 52.1 cm
Courtesy of the People's
History Museum

FIG. 70
FELICITY ASHBEE
(1867–1956)
*They Face Famine in Spain:
They Need Clothes* 1937
Off-set lithograph on paper,
published by the National
Joint Committee for
Spanish Relief
76.3 x 51.6cm
Courtesy of the People's
History Museum

poster in his Ditchling Studios (fig. 67). The studies reveal the development of his ideas from a mass of dispossessed figures, to women and children being fed, and the final design featuring the modern equivalent of the Renaissance 'Madonna of Mercy'. A towering female figure offers protection and comfort to women and children, who cling to her robes before a backdrop of burning buildings. Brangwyn produced the design using the scraperboard technique, in which the black coating of the board is scratched through to reveal the undercoating. The image was converted into a lithographic poster, presumably by R.G. Praill of the Haycock Press, who printed most of Brangwyn's lithographs.

Although similarly focusing on the innocent victims of war, the posters for the Winter Relief fund by Felicity Ashbee (figs. 69–71) feature much more shocking, unsentimental and urgent imagery than Brangwyn's comparatively timeless image. Created in November 1937 the posters all bore the headline 'They Face Famine in Spain', but each had a different focus. Highlighting the need for clothes, one presented a child wrapped in

mended sheets surrounded by silhouetted helping hands; another represented a pale and emaciated brother and sister before the repeated word 'milk'; while a third poster, calling for medical supplies, showed bombs falling around a stricken mother and child – each bomb marked with the words 'Hunger', 'Disease' and 'Desolation', making clear the impact of the Nationalist air raids on civilian targets on the Spanish people.[11] The shocking directness of Ashbee's posters led the London Passenger Transport Board to refuse to display them, deeming them to be too political, and so they were mainly used at public meetings.

Ashbee was the daughter of the socialist Arts and Crafts architect and designer C.R. Ashbee, and she had herself became an ardent Communist Party supporter in the 1930s. In addition to designing posters her cartoons were published in the left-wing weekly political and literary review magazine *Time and Tide*, founded and edited by Margaret, Lady Rhondda. The magazine was a mouthpiece of the feminist 'Six Point Group' and featured contributors such as Eleanor Rathbone,

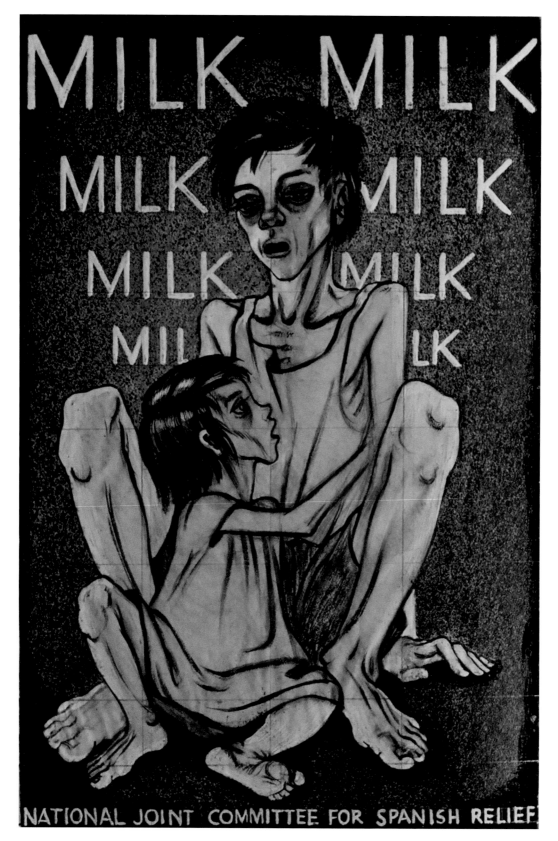

FIG. 71
FELICITY ASHBEE
(1867–1956)
*They Face Famine
in Spain: Milk* 1937
Off-set lithograph on paper,
published by the National
Joint Committee for
Spanish Relief
76.3 x 52 cm
Courtesy of the People's
History Museum

FRANCO : Most surprising ! I have blown the trumpet, and marched round seven times as instructed; and NOTHING happens ! ! There must be something wrong with the trumpet !

FIG. 72
FELICITY ASHBEE
(1867–1956)
Time and Tide, 1936
From Felicity Ashbee's
Record Book
Estate of Felicity Ashbee

FIG. 73
FELICITY ASHBEE
(1867–1956)
Time and Tide, 10 April, 1937
From Felicity Ashbee's
Record Book
Estate of Felicity Ashbee

Naomi Mitchison, Virginia Woolf, Rose Macaulay and Charlotte Haldane. Ashbee's contributions included a prophetic cartoon commenting on the hollowness of the Armistice Commemorations in November 1936 and highlighting how the war in Spain exposed the futility of the lives that were lost in the 'war to end all wars' (fig. 72). Before a dark skyline of bomber planes and searchlights, war profiteers (one carrying a bomb marked 'Spain') lean disrespectfully against the Armistice Memorial ironically inscribed with the words 'LEST WE FORGET'.[12] Another caricature published in April 1937 (fig. 73) made a statement about the Nationalists' inability to take Madrid despite external support. General Franco is shown outside the city walls holding a trumpet marked with 'German and Italian support' under which are the lines: *'FRANCO: Most surprising! I have blown the trumpet and marched round seven times as instructed; and NOTHING happens! There must be something wrong with the trumpet'* (a reference to the Biblical story of the walls of Jericho that fell after Joshua's army marched around the city blowing their trumpets).[13]

Although she was a committed communist, Ashbee's Winter Relief posters had been in support of the nominally non-partisan and largely pacifist National Joint Committee for Spanish Relief, which had been set up in December 1936 as the outcome of a visit of an all-Party group of MPs to Madrid. The committee was formed:

with the object of preventing over-lapping in appeals, of facilitating the allocation of funds and of effecting economies in the despatch of goods to Spain. From the beginning it was agreed that though the organisations as autonomous bodies remained free to give help according to their individual views or preferences, the work of the Joint Committee itself should be purely humanitarian and non-sectarian in character.[14]

The Committee was chaired by the Conservative MP Katherine Stewart-Murray, Duchess of Atholl, supported by the independent MP Eleanor Rathbone and the socialist William Hare, 5th Earl of Listowel, with the Surrealist artist Roland Penrose as Honorary Treasurer. Dubbed the 'Red Duchess' by Lord Rothermere's right-wing press for her backing of the Republican government, she went on a fact-finding trip to Spain with Eleanor Rathbone and Labour MP Ellen Wilkinson in April 1937. In the cities of Valencia, Barcelona and Madrid they observed the impact of Luftwaffe bombing on behalf of the Nationalists, visited prisoners of war held by the Republicans and assessed the effect on women and children, resulting in the Duchess' book *Searchlight on Spain.*

The societies that co-operated with the National Joint Committee for Spanish Relief included a range of humanitarian organisations – the Social Service Council of the Society of Friends, the Save the Children Fund, the Spanish Medical Aid Committee, the Scottish Ambulance Unit, the Spanish Women's Committee for Help to Spain,

the Women's Committee Against War and Fascism, and the Spanish Youth Foodship Committee.[15] The most notable of these was the Spanish Medical Aid Committee (SMAC), formed in August 1936 after Isabel Brown (a communist who was Secretary of the Committee for the Relief of the Victims of Fascism) contacted the Socialist Medical Association about the possibility of sending cross-party medical support to the Republicans.[16] In the words of Peter Spencer, 2nd Viscount Churchill (cousin of Winston Churchill who was the administrator in Spain until mid 1937) 'the Medical Aid Committee soon produced results, and before long we had not only collected medical supplies but also had a team of doctors and trained nurses, ambulance drivers and medical orderlies, all of them volunteers.'[17]

The first British Medical Aid Unit left for Spain on 23 August 1936, sent off by huge crowds at Victoria Station in London. The First British Hospital was established by Kenneth Sinclair Loutit in difficult circumstances at Grañén near Huesca on the Aragon front. At least 150 staff were sent to Spain by the SMAC. Doctors, nurses, administrators and

FIG. 74
Book cover: British Medical *Aid in Spain* Published by the *News Chronicle* The Sherwin Collection

FIG. 75
WINIFRED BATES (1898–1996) *Portrait of Wogan Phillips of the International Brigade holding his pipe and a copy of* Spanish Simplified c.1938, Black and white photograph The International Brigade Archive at the Marx Memorial Library

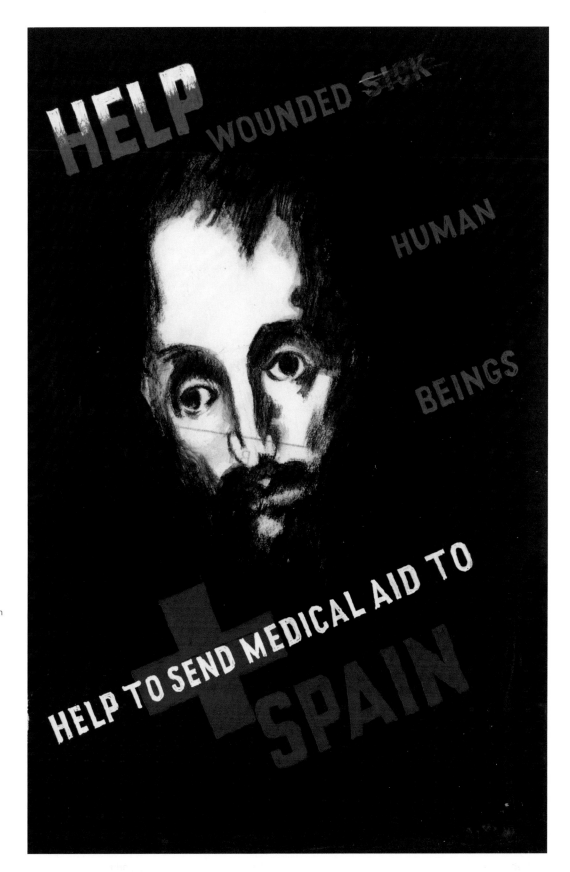

FIG. 76
EDWARD MCKNIGHT
KAUFFER (1899–1954)
Help Wounded Human
Beings: Help to Send
Medical Aid to Spain c.1937
Gouache on paper
57.5 x 42.3
Victoria and Albert Museum

FIG. 77
JOHN F. STEPHENSON (DATES UNKNOWN)
Artists in Bouverie Street, London, painting
a hoarding urging people to support relief action
17 February 1939
Black and white photograph
Topical Press Agency/ Getty Images

ambulance drivers included notable figures such as Winifred Bates, Julian Bell, Archie Cochrane, Nan Green, Reginald Saxton, Thora Silverthorne and Alex Tudor-Hart.[18] Various medical advances were developed as a result of the medical units, including new methods of treating open fractures that led to the reduction in numbers of amputations, new 'triage' techniques that helped in prioritising those needing urgent attention, and revolutionary new techniques for the transfusion of preserved blood in a mobile transfusion unit conceived by Canadian doctor Norman Bethune, supported by Saxton.

The SMAC faced the difficulty of appealing to a broad base of supporters back in England, particularly wealthy patrons whose support was due to humanitarian beliefs rather than sharing the communist conviction of many of those serving in the field. The medical staff experienced horrific scenes in the field, yet for poster designers there remained the problem of creating accessible visual imagery that would generate support for such work without being too visceral. In October 1937 American avant-garde designer E. McKnight Kauffer, who was based in London between 1914 and 1940, designed a poster titled 'Help to Send Medical Aid to Spain' for the SMAC (fig. 76). The poster does not show anything discernibly to do with medical aid, except the red cross symbol, but it is a powerful example of emotive graphic design. The simple and somber image of a man's head was based on El Greco's 'Self-Portrait as St Luke' (c.1604) in the Sacristy of Toledo Cathedral. Whilst the appropriateness of St Luke the Evangelist (who was both an artist and doctor) to an artist's campaign for medical aid was probably lost on many viewers, the pathos of his expression would have made a powerful impact on viewers, underscored by the simple appeal 'HELP WOUNDED HUMAN BEINGS'.

FIG. 78
Ceri Richards and Sam
Haile painting a hoarding in
London, February 1939
Black and white photograph
The Murray Family Collection

Whilst many of these posters were intended to be printed for wider distribution, in February 1939 around 90 members of the AIA created unique illustrated slogans, urging people to support Spanish relief, that were painted directly onto billboards around London. Twenty-two of these had been made available by the London County Council. Although the actual 'posters' were only in place for a couple of weeks, the appeal attracted much coverage in the press, in particular in *Picture Post*. The Surrealists Ceri Richards and Sam Haile were photographed painting a billboard in Hammersmith featuring the Spanish Republican flag emblazoned with the headline: '25000 children have been killed, 50000 are starving in Spain: Send them Food' (figs. 27 and 78). Nan Youngman and Priscilla Thornycroft painted another calling 'Spain fights on: Send food now'. Thornycroft had designed a number of posters, including one for the 'All London Friends of Spain Week' (fig. 79) from 14 to 21 November 1937 that featured a single figure of a peasant farmer holding a bunch of corn.[19] A billboard in Bouverie Street on the theme of foodships

for Spain, a scheme that had been launched in January 1939, attracted interested and sympathetic crowds – as recorded in a press photograph by John F. Stephenson on 17 February 1939 (fig. 77). However, the scheme also provided a focus for Oswald Mosley's 'Blackshirts', who defaced the same billboard with pro-fascist graffiti. As the AIA newsletter in March 1939 reported, 'In addition to giving us the opportunity to demonstrate our support of the unfortunate victims of Fascist methods in Spain, it also gave our native Fascists an opportunity to publicise their own brutal disregard of all human standards, by disfiguring an appeal for starving, defenseless and innocent people'.

Whilst ultimately ephemeral, these poster campaigns were to represent an important step in taking the work of British modern artists out of the elite galleries of the West End of London and into the real world, into direct contact with ordinary, working-class people. In this respect, they did not only send a message concerning democracy and common humanity, but their very form represented a kind of democratisation of art.

FIG. 79
PRISCILLA THORNYCROFT
(b.1917)
*All London Friends
of Spain Week* 1937
Lithograph on paper
75 x 55 cm
Private Collection

FIG. 80
Milk for Spain token issued
as part of fundraising for
Spanish relief in Britain,
c.1936–9, printed card,
The Sherwin Collection

1. Banting, John, 'Notes on Posters of the Spanish Republican Government', in Cyril Connolly (ed.), *Horizon*, vol.11, no.9, September 1940, p.88.
2. In November 1936 the Surrealist poet David Gascoyne had also brought a quantity of Spanish Republican posters back to England from Barcelona for an exhibition at the Whitechapel Art Gallery in aid of supplies for Spain. See David Gascoyne, *Journal 1936–7* (London: Enitharmon, 1978).
3. Banting, *ibid.*, p.88.
4. Ringwood was the home of Bill Alexander, who commanded the British Battalion of the International Brigade.
5. Low 1937, p.226.
6. The slogan inspired the title of a single by the Welsh rock band Manic Street Preachers in 1998, which takes as its theme the idealism of Welsh volunteers who joined the International Brigades to fight against Franco's rebels.
7. Marx Memorial Library, Box 1–2: D/55.
8. George Barker, *Elegy on Spain* (Manchester: The Contemporary Bookshop, April 1939). Printed at the Cloister Press Limited, Heaton Mersey, Manchester.
9. Josep Renau, response to Ramón Gaya's 1937 *Carta de un pintor a un cartelista* (Letter from a Painter to a Poster-artist), cited in Kathleen Vernon (ed.), *The Spanish Civil War and the Visual Arts* (Ithaca, NY: Centre for International

Studies, Cornell University, c.1990).
10. *Glagow Herald*, 9 March 1937.
11. Ashbee's scrapbook features another design marked 'poster in black and red', featuring a vulnerable-looking youth looking up as bomber planes drop bombs around him with the legend 'HELP SPAIN'.
12. On 17 November 1936 during Prime Minister's Questions in the House of Commons 'Mr Mander asked the Prime Minister whether he will consider the advisability of arranging that the Armistice commemoration shall, in future, under present international conditions, take the form of an expression of shame and humiliation at the failure of those now alive to fulfil the purposes for which one million Britons gave their lives in the Great War?'
13. *Time and Tide*, 10 April 1937.
14. National Joint Committee for Spanish Relief, February 1937 (booklet), Archives of the Trades Union Congress, University of Warwick, Ref: 292/946/18b/26.
15. Together with Charlotte Haldane, Ellen Wilkinson and J.B. Priestley, in May 1937 the Duchess of Atholl and Rathbone also established the Dependents Aid Committee, an organisation which raised money for the families of men who were members of the British Battalion in Spain.

16. Dr Christopher Addison was elected president and the Marchioness of Huntingdon agreed to become treasurer. Other supporters included Peter Spencer, Leah Manning, George Jeger, Philip D'Arcy Hart, Frederick Le Gros Clark, Lord Faringdon, Arthur Greenwood, George Lansbury, Victor Gollancz, D.N. Pritt, Archibald Sinclair, Rebecca West, William Temple, Tom Mann, Ben Tillett, Eleanor Rathbone, Julian Huxley, Harry Pollitt and Mary Redfern Davies.
17. Peter Spencer, *All My Sins Remembered*, 1964.
18. For more information on SMAC see Tom Buchanan, 'The Masked Advance: Politics, intrigue and British medical aid for the Spanish Republic', Buchanan 2007, pp 43–63.
19. Thornycroft's brother Christopher had joined the Thälmann Battalion of the International Brigades, serving alongside Winston Churchill's grandson Esmond Romilly at Boadilla in November and December 1936, the Battle of Jarama in February 1937 and in July at Brunete. Her sister Kate was closely involved with the Worthing Committee for Spanish Refugee Children, which supported Beach House in Worthing where 60 Basque children were housed.

5 DREAMING OF SPAIN: The British Surrealist Group Takes Arms

In June 1936, just over a month before the outbreak of the Spanish Civil War, the infamous *International Surrealist Exhibition* opened at the New Burlington Galleries in London. Organised by Roland Penrose, Herbert Read and David Gascoyne, the exhibition featured a remarkable cross-section of Surrealist art – including works by leading European avant-garde artists such as Salvador Dalí, Max Ernst, René Magritte, Joan Miró, Francis Picabia, and Picasso, as well as 23 British artists. At the crowded opening Dylan Thomas walked around offering teacups of boiled string to bemused guests, the Surrealist phantom Sheila Legge wandered through the crowds with her face completely covered with roses, and William Walton hooked a kipper onto a Miró. For those who might dismiss the British Surrealist Group as frivolous and lacking in credibility, Herbert Read gave a speech in which he warned, 'do not judge this movement kindly. It is not just another amusing stunt. It is defiant – the desperate act of men too profoundly convinced of the rottenness of our civilisation to want to save a shred of respectability'.[1]

Despite Read's claims that Surrealism could inspire revolutionary action the Surrealists were subject to abuse from both the British Union of Fascists, who threatened to smash up the exhibition, and the left-wing AIA, to which the group was affiliated and who levelled at them the charge of being too bourgeois. James Boswell featured Read's very words as a quotation on a caricature in the July issue of *Left Review* depicting a group of upper middle-class visitors to the exhibition in their suits and fur coats (fig.83). The AIA held a debate on the occasion of the exhibition at which the communist A.L. Lloyd rejected the political claims of the group, stating that 'if Surrealism were revolutionary, it could be of use. But Surrealism is not revolutionary, because its lyricism is socially irresponsible. Surrealism is a particularly subtle form of fake revolution'.[2] Read himself believed in anarchism, but sought to defend the Marxist orthodoxy of the Surrealists:

I imagine that most of you who have come here tonight if not avowed Socialists or

DECLARATION on SPAIN

Against the appalling mental and physical suffering that the Spanish Civil War is involving, we can already offset certain gains to humanity which will remain whether the Government of the People conquers or not; gains of knowledge which have been purchased far too dearly, but which for that very reason have an imperative claim on our attention. They are these:

1. No one can continue to believe that, if a People's Government is elected constitutionally, Capitalism will be content to oppose it only by constitutional means.

2. No one can continue to believe that violence is the special weapon of the proletariat, while Capitalism is invariably peaceful in its methods.

3. No one can continue to believe that Fascism is a merely national phenomenon. It is now abundantly clear that in a crisis the Fascist countries emerge as parts of an international whole, the International of Capital. German and Italian arms are killing the people of Spain.

4. No one can continue to believe that Fascism cares for or respects what is best in humanity. In García Lorca, the foremost modern poet of Spain, they have assassinated a human life which was especially valuable. Meanwhile the People's Government have made Picasso director of the Prado, hoping to widen still further the scope of his work for humanity.

5. No one can continue to believe that our National Government has any right to speak in the name of democracy. It has assisted in the crime of non-intervention; it has refused to allow the export of arms to a Government democratically constituted, and has regarded with equanimity the assistance given by Fascist powers to the rebels. There can be no more conclusive proof of its real sympathies than its conduct towards Portugal. Portugal is a British financial colony, and depends on British arms for the protection of its overseas possessions. A word from our Foreign Office would have secured her immediate adherence to the pact of non-intervention. Evidently that word has not been given. The National Government has permitted the Portuguese dictatorship to assist the rebels in complete freedom; at every stage of the campaign the rebel armies have been based on the Portuguese frontier.

If these things are clear, we are the gainers in so far as we know *inescapably* where we stand with regard to Fascism, to the People's Government, and to the National Government of Britain. And in the light of this knowledge we support the popular demand that the ban on the export of arms to the Spanish Government be lifted. We accuse our National Government of duplicity and anti-democratic intrigue, and call upon it to make at once the only possible reparation

ARMS
for the People of Spain

Hugh Sykes Davies, David Gascoyne, Humphrey Jennings, Diana Brinton Lee, Rupert Lee, Henry Moore, Paul Nash, Roland Penrose, Valentine Penrose, Herbert Read, Roger Roughton.

Farleigh Press (T.U.), E.C.1   ISSUED BY THE SURREALIST GROUP IN ENGLAND.

Do not judge this movement kindly. It is not just another amusing stunt. It is defiant—the desperate act of men too profoundly convinced of the rottenness of our civilisation to want to save a shred of its respectability. HERBERT READ.

Surrealist Exhibition London 1936

Communists, have at any rate revolutionary sympathies. It seems paradoxical therefore that I should be expected to speak in defence of revolutionary art ... I speak for an art that is uncompromisingly aggressive. It is for others to explain why in this domain of thought and feeling, we who are revolutionaries should respect the established order of things ... The culture of the whole capitalist epoch is poisoned with its own particular virus and no part of that culture is so rotten and ridiculous as that latter day convention of Realism.[3]

The outbreak of the Spanish Civil War was to give the British Surrealists a particular focus over the coming years, inspiring them to issue manifestos, to take part in marches and exhibitions, and participate in debates about Spain and politics. As Julian Trevelyan later recalled:

that hot summer, a few weeks after the exhibition had closed, the Spanish Civil War broke out, and for the next three years our thoughts

and consciences were turned to Spain. Dali immediately christened a great picture on which he had been working *Prémonitions de la Guerre Civil Espagnol,* and it was against a background of uncanalised desire for some sort of militant action to stop the spread of Fascism that our little Surrealist group formed and functioned.[4]

The fourth number of the *International Surrealist Bulletin* issued by the Surrealist group in England in September 1936 stated that:

the movement of our government towards Fascism threatens to put a stop to all creative activity .... Against this it is absolutely necessary to combine, to force a dialectical solution of a series of existing conflicts: reality with the dream, society with the individual, the ideology of the artist with his creative activity. This is to be done by attacking the problems of art and society by means of a coherent activity which will secure the creative transformation of life itself.[5]

FIG. 82
Declaration on Spain by the Surrealist Group in England, inserted in *Contemporary Poetry and Prose,* November 1936, Printed by the Farleigh Press, The Sherwin Collection

FIG. 83
JAMES BOSWELL (1906–71)
Surrealist Exhibition, London 1936, Drawing, reproduced in *Left Review,* July 1936 Collection of Ruth Boswell

Roland Penrose had strong links to the European Surrealists and in the summer of 1936 he and his wife Valentine were invited to stay in Mougins in the South of France by the Surrealist poet Paul Éluard and his wife Nusch. They were joined by other friends including Picasso and his new partner Dora Maar, the editor of *Cahiers d'Art* Christian Zervos and his wife Yvonne, and Man Ray. Penrose later recalled that the news of fighting in Spain had caused them all 'agonising misgivings', and that hearing reports in the press of vandalism and rioting in Catalonia being blamed on the anarchists caused Zervos to decide, 'that he must see for himself if this were true or just another Fascist attempt to make the Spanish Republic appear incompetent and under the thumb of left-wing extremists'.[6] Penrose offered to accompany him 'with a view to bringing back to London an eye-witness account of the situation'.[7] As seen in chapter 1, from October to December of that year Penrose, Zervos and their wives toured heritage sites in towns and cities in Catalonia including Barcelona, Vic, Gerona, Lérida, Tarragona and Valencia, together with the Surrealist poet David Gascoyne and others. Penrose took numerous photographs, some recording the group in various locations (including Valentine sporting a glamorous leopard-skin coat greatly unsuited to a war zone), and documenting street processions of anarchist organisations and trade unions, damage to buildings from artillery fire, and troops in training camps. He recalled that a visit to Picasso's mother in Barcelona was to 'challenge my hope that all was well' after she explained she was only able then to open her window after several days of asphyxiating smoke and stench from a burning convent nearby.

Returning to London, Penrose brought with him with photographs from the front by Hungarian war photographer Robert Capa. His return in December 1936 coincided with W.H. Auden writing to the scholar Professor Eric Dodds of his plan to join the International Brigades in Spain, in which he expressed a view that was symptomatic of the weariness and suspicion with which the Surrealists were seen by the Left: 'I so dislike everyday political activities that I won't do them, but here is something I can do as a citizen and not as a writer, and as I have no

dependents, I feel I ought to go; but O I do hope there are not too many Surrealists there.'[8]

Whilst in Barcelona David Gascoyne had worked in the Propaganda Ministry 'translating news bulletins during the day, and broadcasting them, in English, from a studio in the Ministry of Marine, near the post, every evening at 6 o'clock'.[9] In his autobiography *World Within World* Stephen Spender recalled how, 'one evening when I was in the main square, I heard a rather languid English voice broadcasting from loudspeakers attached to the eighth-story windows of a building above me. Listening hard, I suddenly recognised it as that of the poet David Gascoyne'.[10] Before leaving for Spain Gascoyne had joined the British Communist Party, even carrying the banner of the Twickenham branch at the demonstration against Mosley's Union of British Fascists in Alexandra Park in London. Yet he later recalled that in Barcelona he, 'came to find that the Communists hated the Anarchists and the P.O.U.M. (Trotskyists) much more than they hated the Fascists, and I think this was the beginning of my disillusionment with Communism as a means of creating a better world'.[11]

The Surrealists' concern about their position in relation to the fundamental difference of ideology between the political philosophies of Stalinist Communism and Trotskyist Anarchism was a reflection of the acute situation in Spain, where Stalinists and anarchists were actually fighting each other despite being nominally on the same side. In September 1936 the Surrealist poet Roger Roughton had declared that: 'Surrealist work, while not calling directly for revolutionary intervention, can be classed as revolutionary insofar as it can break down irrational bourgeois-taught practices, thus preparing mental ground for positive revolutionary thought and action ... as long as the surrealists will help to establish a broad United Front.'[12] To some extent they moved towards this with a 'Declaration on Spain' (fig. 82) that was included in the November 1936 issue of Roughton's *Contemporary Poetry and Prose*, in which they stated their political position and opposition to the British government's policy of non-intervention. It was signed by the leading artists and poets in the movement – Hugh Sykes Davies, Gascoyne,

On the occasion of the Artists' International Congress and Exhibition

WE ASK YOUR ATTENTION

NON-INTERVENTION is not merely a political expedient in the Spanish situation, nor the alleged policy of a certain international committee. It is something much more than that; it is the typical and inevitable product of a way of thinking and behaving, the prevailing political attitude of **educated and conscious** people since the war.

This attitude has been pure NON-INTERVENTION. Politics were looked upon as a dirty and stupid game of little real importance. Politicians were paid off to play it on their own, recognised knaves and professional liars, but not too sharply questioned as long as things went not too outrageously, and above all as long as the intellectuals were left safely with their books, their arts and intellectual interests. Their aim was to localise politics, to confine it to a few people, to treat it as a possibly contagious, certainly disgusting disease.

This attitude has been modified in one direction only. Memories of the last war, and the obviously growing dangers of another, have produced widespread pacifism. For the pacifist tries to deal with war as an isolated disaster, apart from its wider causes and connections; he tries to look upon it as the embodiment of an abstract principle of VIOLENCE, and he will try to oppose it by the usually abstract principle of REASON. He will not examine the actual social and economic circumstances which produce violence, and above all he will not seek to oppose it by actual political means; he will not meet it on its own ground. He remains NON-INTERVEN-TIONIST.

In a similar way the London Non-Intervention Committee was designed to apply this policy in the situation created by the international Fascist coup in Spain. Political expedience and political justice were ignored; all social and political circumstances were disregarded, in favour of a single object: to localise the conflict, to confine within limits as narrow as possible the outbreak of VIOLENCE.

In this way the London Committee has a significance far beyond its own immediate aims. It is a practical test, a crucial experiment upon the attitudes which we have adopted. Is it possible to remain blind any longer to the rest of the experiment?

The facts, the events, are not in dispute. The Fascist countries, Italy, Germany and Portugal, have assisted Franco freely with materials of war and barely disguised divisions of their regular armies. They have condescended to cloak their actions to some extent under promises, agreements, denials and counter-charges. But behind this fog of words, Fascist intervention has proceeded unhampered save by the magnificent courage of the armies of THE SPANISH PEOPLE.

Is there any reason to suppose that Non-Intervention at future times and in other places may succeed better? Has Fascist militarism announced any limit to its hopes of conquest? Has it shown signs of a moral regeneration, of a greater respect for agreements and conventions? The opinion of the politicians at least is clear. Since the Fascist outbreak in Spain every European country has hastened and enlarged its plans of re-armament. Only a few pacifists continue to believe in Non-Intervention. By doing so, they can only assist the forces of war by yielding one strategic point after another to militarist dictators, they make VIOLENCE more certain and infinitely more disastrous in its effects.

One thing, then, is clear. With all respect for the motives of pacifism, for the sincerity and courage of pacifists, this form of Non-Intervention is completely discredited in practice by the Spanish experiment. But more depends on the experiment than this. Not only pacifism has been on trial, but our whole attitude of Non-Intervention in politics. How have our paid knaves and liars conducted themselves? Unfortunately, like paid knaves and liars. If, conceivably, six months ago NON-INTERVENTION was defensible, it was only remotely justifiable as long as there was a fair fight between the parties in Spain. The German and Italian invasions removed even these remote justifications. At the very least we might have expected unequivocal protests against the Fascist aggressors, but even these have been lacking.

Unfortunately, this is not all. Our Government has in various ways intervened actually on behalf of the Fascist aggressors. Several weeks before the international ban on volunteers, it dug up a century-old Act on Foreign Enlistment, and indicated its intention to harass British volunteers gratuitously by this antiquated instrument. It has repeatedly refused to admit representatives of THE SPANISH PEOPLE, and their

FIG. 84
Surrealist Declaration on the Occasion of the Artists' International Congress and Exhibition with a motif by Henry Moore (1898–1986), 1937, Printed by the Farleigh Press, The Sherwin Collection

FIG. 85
HENRY MOORE (1898–1986)
Arms for Spain - Cover for
*Contemporary Poetry and
Prose*, 10, Autumn 1937
1937
Off-set lithograph
in bound book
21.5 x 14 cm
Private Collection, Brighton

Humphrey Jennings, Diana Brinton Lee, Rupert Lee, Henry Moore, Paul Nash, Roland and Valentine Penrose, Read and Roughton. In it they stated:

we know *inescapably* where we stand with regard to Fascism, to the People's Government, and to the National Government of Britain. And in the light of this knowledge we support the popular demand that the ban on the export of arms to the Spanish Government be lifted. We accuse our National Government of duplicity and anti-democratic intrigue, and call upon it to make at once the only possible reparation ARMS for the People of Spain.

The magazine's editorial by Roughton claimed that the conflict in Spain highlighted the violent nature of international capital: 'No one can continue to believe that Fascism cares for or respects what it is best in humanity. In García Lorca the foremost poet of Spain, they have assassinated a human life which was especially valuable.'[13] Despite their direct statement on Spain, the Surrealists' 'subjective

interests' received further criticism in *Left Review*, with A.L. Lloyd welcoming their statement but asserting that automatic writing and the belief in chance would never 'make the proletariat conscious of its social and revolutionary responsibilities'.[14]

In spring 1937 the exhibition *Unity of Artists for Peace, for Democracy, for Cultural Progress*, organised by the AIA at Grosvenor Square in London to coincide with the Artists International Congress, featured a room assigned to the Surrealists with its own selection jury. In addition to leading international figures such as Dalí, Delvaux, Ernst, Giacometti, Klee, Miró, Picasso, Man Ray and Tanguy, the Surrealist section presented the work of numerous English artists including John Banting, Sam Haile, Moore, Nash, John Tunnard, and F.E. McWilliam, and the Australian James Cant. Out of a total of 1000 works in the rather incoherent exhibition 118 were Surrealist, of which 43 were by British artists. To mark the Artists International Congress and the exhibition the Surrealists issued a broadsheet entitled 'We Ask Your Attention', which featured a bold red abstract motif over the text designed by Henry Moore (fig.84). The broadsheet was given to visitors to the exhibition and sought to highlight the Surrealists' opposition to the British government's policy of non-intervention in Spain, asserting the view that:

> We no longer have any excuse. NON-INTERVENTION in all forms must end. Artists, intellectuals, all people who live consciously, must recognise their political responsibilities, above all, their duty of direct political action in defence of their own interests. Do not let us deceive ourselves further; in a militarised state the activities we value, the kind of consciousness which produces them, cannot exist.

Quoting William Blake's aphorism 'A warlike state cannot create' they highlighted how, 'setting aside general questions of democracy, justice, humanity, we are forced to defend the bare opportunity to carry on our work'. This call for intervention sought to emphasise common interests over individual views and shared ground with organisations such as the Association of Writers for the Defence of Culture and the movement for a United Front. Asserting Surrealism's unique position, it ended with the call to:

> INTERVENE IN THE FIELD OF POLITICS, INTERVENE IN THE FIELD OF THE IMAGINATION. THE REVOLUTION which we can bring about must have as its object the DEVELOPMENT OF CONSCIOUSNESS and the WIDER SATISFACTION OF DESIRE. Economic justice is the first object of our intervention, but we demand also the vindication of the psychological rights of man, the liberation of intelligence and imagination. INTERVENE AS POETS, ARTISTS AND INTELLECTUALS BY VIOLENT OF SUBTLE INVERSION AND BY STIMULATING DESIRE.

The list of signatories included the architect Erno Goldfinger, the artists Eileen Agar, Norman Dawson, Merlyn Evans, George Graham, Charles Howard, Rupert Lee, Moore, Paul Nash, Penrose, and Trevelyan, and the poets Hugh Sykes Davies, Gascoyne, and Read.

Given the directness of their appeal, much of the artwork created by the Surrealists at this time was more expressive of 'subtle inversion' than a direct intervention. Penrose's collage *Elephant Bird* (fig. 86) could be interpreted as a subconscious or associational response to the war, but it would be hard to identify a particular message. The collaged section of a map of Catalonia which forms part of the 'elephant bird' of the title includes the regions around Barcelona that Penrose had visited in the autumn of 1936, whilst the multiple postcards of the Eiffel Tower and Sacre Coeur in Paris repeated in a column to create a metamorphic form would have had associations with the Paris Worlds Fair (where the tower stood at the centre). Much of the criticism that was levelled against Picasso's *Guernica* when it was shown at the Paris Worlds Fair, and in the subsequent showings in Britain organised by Penrose and Read in the autumn of 1938 and early 1939, had been that its 'message' could not be readily understood outside of an artistic elite (see chapter 6). In January 1938 the *Artists News Sheet* featured a review by Jack Chen complaining that the 'bad influence of expressionism, surrealism, futurism and abstractionism are still too much in evidence',[15] and of his incomprehension of Picasso's work. This prompted an immediate reaction from 13 of the Surrealists in the next issue – including Agar, Cant, Haile, F.E. McWilliam, Moore, Ceri Richards, Penrose and Trevelyan – in which they threatened to withdraw from the AIA if that was its official attitude. This drew an apology from AIA in which it recognised the Surrealists' 'efficacy' and a statement that the theory on which an artist 'may base his work, does not affect his status as a member'.[16]

On 16 March 1938 the AIA held a public debate between the Surrealists and Realists at the Group Theatre Rooms in London. Representing the Surrealists were Penrose, Trevelyan and Jennings; for the Realists were Graham Bell, William Coldstream and émigré sculptor Peter Peri. 'Stuck up behind the speakers were examples of the two schools. I confess that the work of my friends, honest to goodness enough and intelligent, looked pretty dull there,' recalled figurative painter William Townsend. 'The others had the unfair advantage of a Picasso and a Miró! The Surrealists, too, were

FIG. 86
ROLAND PENROSE
(1900–84)
Elephant Bird 1938
Collage with paper and string
93 x 70 cm
Victoria and Albert Museum

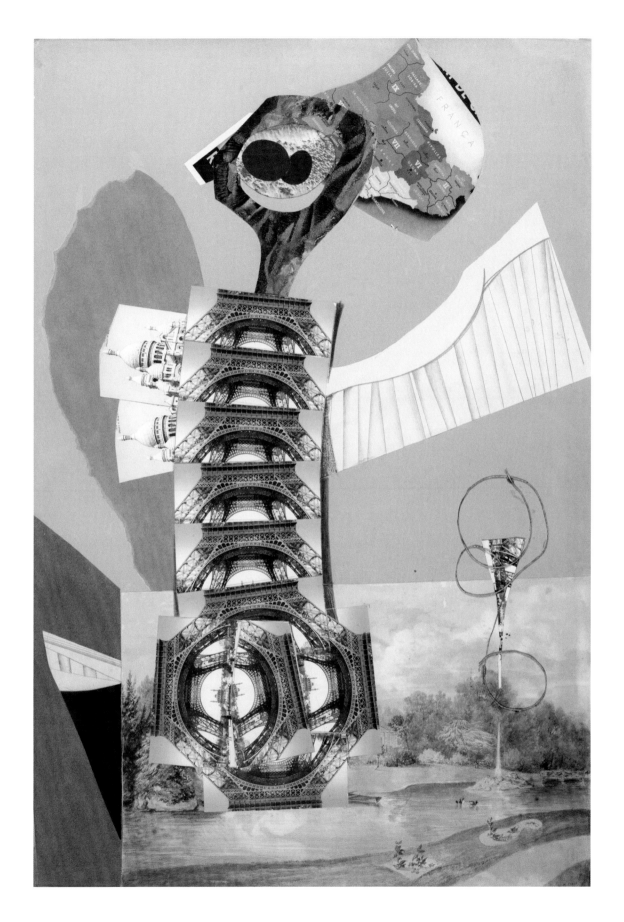

FIG. 87
HENRY MOORE (1898–1986)
Five Figures in a Setting 1937
Charcoal (rubbed), pastel
(washed), crayon on paper
38 x 55.5 cm
The Henry Moore Family
Collection

by far the more brilliant, fluent and well-prepared team of debaters, and Penrose was really quite successful in calling forth the merits of his favoured exhibits.'[17] Reporting the event in the *London Bulletin*, the fortnightly Surrealist magazine issued by the London Gallery, Read scornfully observed that 'actually our English realists are not the tough guys that ought to be but the effete and bastard offspring of the Bloomsbury school of needlework'.[18]

In artworks created around this time bridging figuration, abstraction and Surrealism, such as *Five Figures in a Setting* (fig.87), Henry Moore was expressing an atmosphere of threat and containment that can be seen to obliquely relate to his concerns about Spain which ultimately leads to his *Spanish Prisoner* drawing and print in 1939 (fig. 142 and 1, see chapter 7). Moore attempted to travel out to Spain in January 1938 with Jacob Epstein, but was denied a visa by the British government. Whilst his Republican sympathies were clear from his design for the broadsheet and the slogan 'ARMS FOR SPAIN' that accompanied his cover design for *Contemporary Poetry and Prose 10* in Autumn

1937 (fig. 85), there was nothing in the imagery itself that could be viewed as expressing a directly legible statement on politics. Aside from the use of the same colour blue there is no discernable thematic connection between his nine abstracted figures and the notion of sending arms to Spain.

Similarly, there appears to be a disjunction between the violent and suggestive title of Merlyn Evans' painting *Torturing the Anarchist* (fig. 88) and the almost hermetic and moth-like abstract form depicted in the painting.[19] Evans painted numerous works peopled with abstracted humanoids in the 1930s and 1940s, which relate to themes such as the Italian occupation of Abyssinia, the Russian invasion of Finland and the bombing of Guernica (see *Distressed Area*, fig. 121, chapter 6 and *Tyrannopolis,* fig. 124, chapter 6). There are affinities to the work of Wyndham Lewis whom he admired stylistically, but their politics were widely divergent, with Evans being firmly to the Left, although he disliked joining any artists' or political groups. Anarchism had gained more support and influence in Spain during

FIG. 88
MERLYN EVANS (1910–73)
Torturing the Anarchist
1937/8
Tempera on canvas
48 x 37 cm
Estate of Merlyn Evans

the Civil War than anywhere else, particularly in the form of urban anarcho-syndicalism in Barcelona. In 1934 the anarchist CNT had organised a miners' strike in Asturias, which had been brutally crushed by Franco, with captured miners facing torture, mutilation and execution, and it may be this to which Evans alludes.

During the Civil War the communists and liberals sought to crush the anarchist revolution, but sympathy for the ideas of anarchism was manifested in works by Surrealists such as Eileen Agar's sculpture the *Angel of Anarchy* (1937), which featured in the exhibition *Surrealist Objects and Poems* at the London Gallery in November 1937. Another sculpture in the same exhibition was Peter Norman Dawson's *British Diplomacy* (1937, lost) constructed from seemingly random objects (a syringe, hook and doll) fixed to a wooden fish to create a ludicrous assemblage. In 1938 Herbert Read published his book *Poetry and Anarchism* in which he wrote of his belief that, 'In Spain, and almost only in Spain, there still lives a spirit to resist the bureaucratic tyranny

of the State and the intellectual intolerance of all doctrinaires. For that reasons all poets must follow the course of this struggle with open and passionate partisanship'.[20] Read contributed to the anarchist fortnightly magazine *Spain and the World,* which was published between December 1936 and December 1938, and included his poem *A Song for Spanish Anarchists:*

The golden lemon is not made
but grows on a green tree:
A strong man and his crystal eyes
is a man born free.

The oxen pass under the yoke
and the blind are led at will:
But a man born free has a path of his own
and a house on the hill.

And men are men who till the land
and women are women who weave
Fifty men own the lemon grove
and no man is a slave.[21]

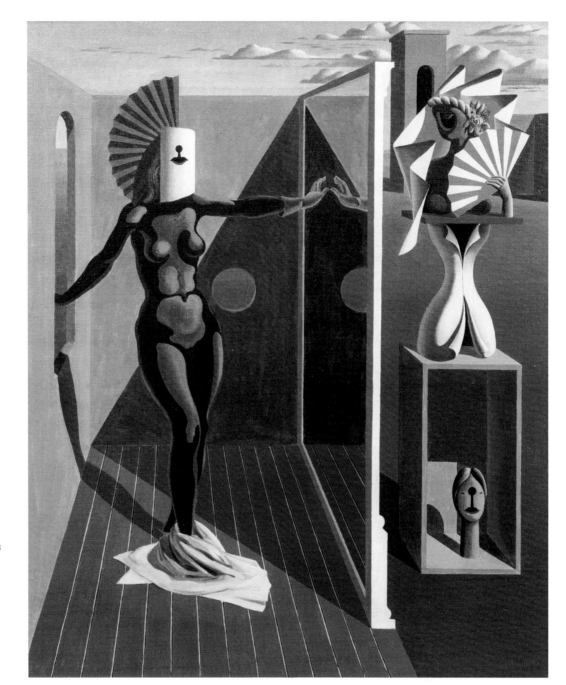

FIG. 89
COLIN MIDDLETON
(1910–83)
Spain Dream Revisited 1938
Oil on canvas
61 x 51 cm
Private collection courtesy
of Karen Reihill Fine Art

FIG. 90
COLIN MIDDLETON
(1910–83)
The Bride 1938
Oil on canvas
61 x 51 cm
Private collection courtesy
of Karen Reihill Fine Art

The Irish Surrealist Colin Middleton remained entirely separate from these debates and the debates of the British Surrealists, considering himself to be the only Surrealist working in Ireland during the 1930s. Trained at Belfast College of Art and working principally as a damask designer he looked directly to the European Surrealists, particularly the metaphysical paintings of Dalí. Middleton was fascinated by Jung's concept of the female archetype, which he explored in psychologically charged paintings such as *The Bride* (fig. 90) and *Spain Dream Revisited* (fig. 89) – in which a crucified female nude sits within a red framework on a table, approached by a faceless nun in stylised black robes in a room looking out onto a Spanish townscape. Whether or not this is an anti-clerical statement is unclear.

Subtlety was not an issue in John Banting's savage drawing *Absolution: Spanish Civil War* (fig. 91), a biting comment on what was perceived to be the hypocritical and complicit role of the Catholic church during the conflict. A committed communist as well as a Surrealist, Banting had travelled to Spain with Nancy Cunard from October to December

1937, visiting first Barcelona, then Valencia (where they met the American poet Langston Hughes), and subsequently Madrid, where Banting had unsuccessfully attempted to join the International Brigades. In Banting's drawing a priest is depicted carrying out prayers of absolution for the dead victims that surround him, and yet the implication is that this monstrous skull-headed priest bearing weapons and the symbol of the fasces is actually responsible for their deaths. The French Surrealist André Masson had explored a similar theme in *La Messe à Pampelone (Mass in Pamplona)* (fig.92), in which priests with skeletal heads appear behind an asinine bishop who offers communion wafers marked with the swastika. The drawing was a satire on the fact that the Bishop of Pamplona had described the war as 'the loftiest crusade that the centuries have ever seen … a crusade in which divine intervention on our side is evident' in a sermon of August 1936.[22] Later, having denounced the Republicans as 'the enemies of God and Spain', he had offered to grant indulgences to anyone who killed a Marxist. The hypocrisy of the Catholic

FIG. 91
JOHN BANTING (1902–72)
Absolution: Spanish Civil War
c.1937–9
Red ink on paper
mounted on board
25.4 x 19.1 cm
Collection Adrian Dannatt,
New York

FIG. 92
ANDRÉ MASSON
(1896–1987)
*La Messe à Pampelone
(Mass in Pamplona)* 1937
Ink and pencil on paper
80 x 97 cm
The Sherwin Collection

church was a common theme, also explored by the poet Stanley Richardson in 'To a Common Priest':

'I have no time for you', this preacher said,
And turned his pen to propagating lies.
About war's victims, and the martyred dead
He wrote with gusto vile; and closed his eyes
On Guernica and bloody Badajoz
On you, Madrid, Life's glorious capital:
He wrote for tyranny, ignoring truth,
And praised to Heaven Franco's Fascist Hell.

God in that day when proof is read,
Show all thy charity to this poor priest
Who basely wore the livery of thy Son
Thy mercy on the traiter's tonsured head,
Who heaped his cruel message on thy least
And served the rich, and knew it, and sinned on.

Debunking pretensions of grandeur and political hegemony through satirical and absurdist gestures was a particular strategy of the Surrealists. The Surrealists' participation in the 1938 May Day

Parade in Hyde Park formed one of the most memorable political actions made by any artistic group. Trevelyan recalled that they had been 'determined to make a splash'. They hired a van on which they installed a loudspeaker that played the communist 'Internationale' and Spanish Republican records, with a cage in which hung a skeleton. This was followed by an ice-cream tricycle on which they rigged a structure of wire-netting filled with coloured balloons and topped by a white horse's head, made by Trevelyan (fig. 95). F.E. McWilliam had made four papier-mâché masks of Prime Minister Neville Chamberlain and James Cant, T Graham, Penrose and Trevelyan appeared dressed as Chamberlain, complete with top hats and umbrellas. 'We marched along together shouting, "Chamberlain must go"', recalled Trevelyan. 'It was a day of cold east wind and I was soon hoarse with shouting, but on the whole I think we added something effective to the *cortége*. Occasionally, when the procession stopped, we danced a little minuet together, waving our umbrellas.'[23]

FIG. 93
FE MCWILLIAM (1909–92)
Mask of Neville Chamberlain
for May Day Procession
1938
Painted papier-mâché
19 x 12 cm
The Murray Family
Collection

FIG. 94
Photograph of the Surrealist artists Roland Penrose, James Cant, Julian Trevelyan and T.Graham wearing masks of Prime Minister Neville Chamberlain made by McWilliam in the May Day Procession, 1938.

FIG. 95
JULIAN TREVELYAN
(1910–88)
Horse's head from the Surrealist float at the May Day Procession 1938
Painted papier-mâché
14.7 x 19.9 cm
Courtesy of the
Trevelyan Estate

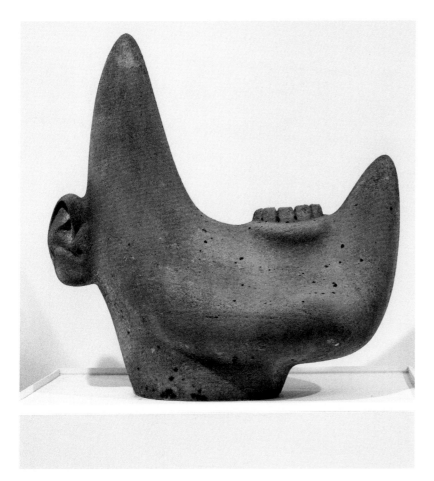

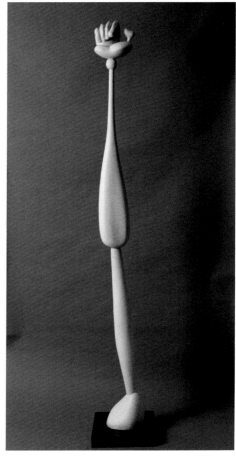

F.E. McWilliam created some of the most overtly symbolic Surrealist responses to the Spanish Civil War. In addition to his tragic sculptures *Spanish Head* (fig. 120, chapter 6) and *Mandible* (fig. 96), which drew on the imagery of Picasso's *Guernica* (see chapter 6), he also created a sculpture entitled *The Long Arm* (fig. 97). This white limewood sculpture forms a totemic icon, and may have been informed by the spatial qualities of Alberto Sánchez Pérez's sculpture *The Spanish People Have a Path that Leads to a Star* (1937), which stood outside the Spanish Republican Pavilion at the Paris Worlds Fair in 1937. The clenched fist formed the Loyalist Salute and was a symbol of anti-fascism, since the ideal symbolised by the clenched fist was shared by all political and social groups in the Republic (whether anarchist, socialist or communist). McWilliam later remarked, 'the idea of that Long Arm with a hand on the top was the popular front salute, the clenched fist. Actually my fist isn't quite clenched because ... I was only a fellow traveller'.[24] The defiant gesture was also the basis of Miró's print *Aidez L'Espagne* (*Help Spain*) (fig. 98) in

which a Catalan peasant raises their clenched fist in the Loyalist salute. It was originally designed as a 1 franc stamp, to be sold in France to benefit the Republican Government in Spain, but the stamp was never issued. Instead Miró made a pochoir stencil print which was printed in two editions, one of which included a lithographed inscription in handwriting:

> In this present battle I see on the fascist side just the outdated forces, and on the other side, the people whose immense creative resources which will give Spain a power which will astonish the whole world.

The *Solidarité* portfolio involving a number of Surrealists was another fundraising initiative, printed in an edition of 150 and sold to aid the Spanish Republican Children's Fund. It was published by Editions G.L.M. (poet and publisher Guy Lévis Mano) to accompany a signed poem by Paul Éluard entitled *November 1936*, which was translated by the Irish poet Brian Coffey. The poem took its title from the month in which the rebel troops launched a relentless

FIG. 96
FE MCWILLIAM (1909–92)
Mandible 1938
Hoptonwood stone
60cm
Private Collection, England

FIG. 97
FE MCWILLIAM (1909–92)
The Long Arm 1939
Lime wood
185 cm high
The Sherwin Collection

FIG. 98
JOAN MIRÓ (1893–1983)
Aidez L'Espagne
(Help Spain) 1937
Pochoir with lithographic
inscription on paper
31.3 x 24.5 cm
The Sherwin Collection

bombardment of Madrid but failed to take the city. Featuring four engravings and three etchings, the portfolio included a Miró abstract with a crescent moon, a Picasso head of a woman in profile with a beret, a macabre André Masson of a metamorphic dove weeping tears of blood and fusing with the land, its claw-like foot suggesting a tree, and other prints by Dalla Husband, Yves Tanguy, John Buckland Wright and S.W. Hayter. The portfolio was printed in Paris by Henri Hecht at Atelier 17, the avant-garde print studio run by Hayter. One of the most influential British printmakers in the twentieth-century Hayter was a key figure in the Surrealist movement.[25] He worked with many of the international avant-garde including Victor Brauner, Ernst, Giacometti, Masson, Miró, Tanguy and Raoul Ubac. Atelier 17 formed an important meeting point and bridge between British and international artists in the 1930s. Many British artists who had been drawn to Paris arrived at Atelier 17, including Agar, Banting, Conroy Maddox, Penrose and Trevelyan – whose etching *Spain 1936* (fig. 99) reveals the impact of meeting Alexander Calder and Miró whilst at Atelier 17.

S.W. Hayter had begun sketches for a large etching called *Combat* in April 1936, but did not complete the plate until the end of that year, telling a friend that 'it was sort of prophetic, as the Spanish war started in July that year'.[26] He went to Spain for four months from September 1937 at the invitation of the Ministry of Arts of the Republican government. He slipped across the border with safe conduct papers, visiting amongst other places Barcelona and Madrid, where he saw the new edition of Goya's *The Disasters of War* being printed (see chapter 1), and recording prisons, batteries, trenches and schools in paintings and drawings that were exhibited at the Mayor Gallery in February 1938. Hayter reported that the Republicans were 'busy and bustling with a hundred and one cultural activities that they were not able to indulge in the old days'.[27]

A number of boldly coloured, abstract paintings resulted from his trip to Spain including *Plaza Nationale* (1937), *Evacuados* (fig 100), *Ramblas* (fig. 101), which was presumably named after the avenue in Barcelona, and *Fuerteduena* (1937), named

FIG. 99
JULIAN TREVELYAN
(1910–88)
Spain 1936 (printed 1972)
Gouache and intaglio print on paper
15.6 x 25.4 cm
Courtesy of Bohun Gallery, Henley on Thames

FIG. 100
S.W. HAYTER (1901–88)
Evacuados 1937
Oil and gouache on panel
26.5 x 20 cm
Private Collection, France

FIG. 101
S.W. HAYTER (1901–88)
Ramblas 1937
Oil and gouache on panel
32 x 19 cm
Private Collection, France

after a village in Segovia 25 miles from the Jarama battleground which featured in Jorge Ivens' 1937 documentary film *The Spanish Earth* (narrated by Ernst Hemingway). Tragic figurative elements within these paintings, and the related etchings, serve to express suffering and violence – in the foreground of *Paysage Anthropophage (Man-eating Landscape)* (fig. 102) and the etching of the same subject a dead figure lies with his arm outstretched, before a stricken female figure, and in *Douro* the same female lies vanquished on a riverbank. The subject was based on the play *The Siege of Numantia* by sixteenth-century Spanish author Miguel de Cervantes, which centred on the destruction of a Spanish city by the Romans in 133 BC. This had obvious thematic connections to the role of the fascists in modern Spain. In the play the symbolic female river goddess Duoro stands on the banks of the river to express her lamentation for the city in a patriotic outburst. The play includes scenes of destruction, mass suicide and famine, and ends with the allegorical figure of Fame announcing the future glory of Spain. Hayter

produced four prints including the aforementioned prints, plus *Defeat* and *Runner* (fig. 105) to accompany the text in a new publication to be published by French publisher and dealer Ambrose Vollard – but his death in 1939 meant that Hayter had to publish the prints individually. *Runner* was printed both on paper and two impressions on plaster, one included here. Hayter was also to create prints to be sold to support the Spanish Republican Children's Fund, such as a greeting card for 1937–8 titled *Ayuda a España* (fig. 103) .

In 1939 Hayter printed a follow-up portfolio to *Solidarit*é, which was entitled *Fraternité*, also in support of Spanish Civil War relief, to accompany the poem *Fall of a City* by Stephen Spencer (translated into French by Louis Aragon). The portfolio comprised ten engravings, including a slipcase cover, by artists including Joseph Hecht, Dalla Husband, Wassily Kandinsky, Roderick Mead, Miró, Dolf Reiser, Luis Vargas and Buckland Wright, together with Hayter's *España*. In the poem Spender expresses the sadness of Republican defeat:

FIG. 102
STANLEY WILLIAM HAYTER (1901–88)
Paysage Anthropophage (Man-eating Landscape) 1937
Oil on panel
100 x 200cm
Private Collection, France

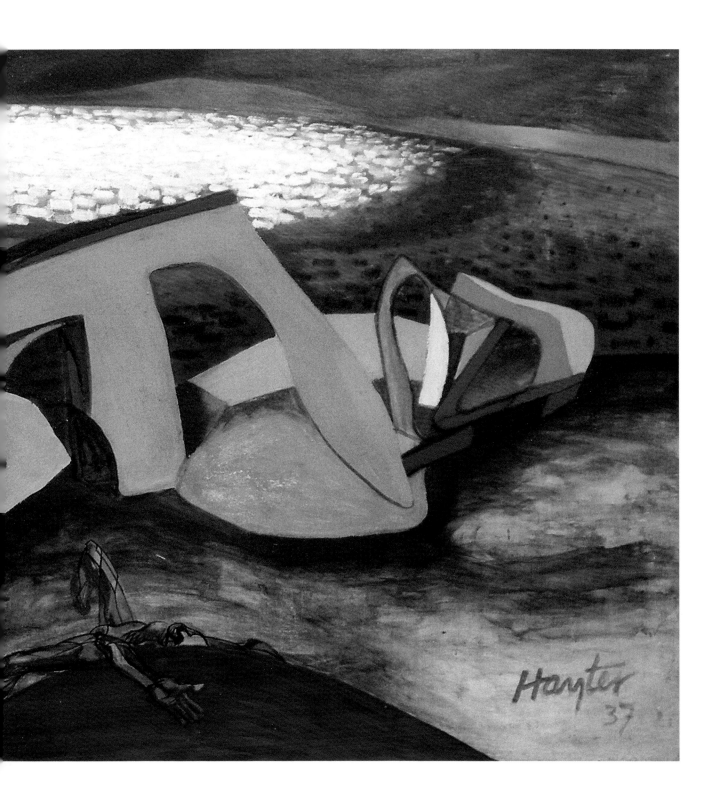

Ayuda a España

All the posters on the walls
All the leaflets in the streets
Are mutilated, destroyed or run in rain
Their words blotted out with tears
Skin peeling from their bodies
In the victorious hurricane.

And yet it ends with the suggestion of an
enduring spirit of freedom in spite of defeat:

Some old man's memory jumps to a child
- Spark from the days of energy.
And the child hoards it like a bitter toy.

The relationship between the British and European
Surrealists over their political allegiances to Stalinist
Marxism, or Trotsykyism, was increasingly strained
after the issuing of 'Towards an Independent
Revolutionary Art' by André Breton and Diego
Rivera in 1938 (which Breton is believed to have
written with Trotsky). This was followed by Breton's
letter 'To Our Friends in London' sent in October
1938, in which he asserted his view that the British
Surrealist Group must define its position towards
Trotskyism: 'Certain surrealists in London, it appears,
hesitate. We hope that this letter will help them to
dispel their fears. If this not the case, it is obvious
that they will only be surrealists in name. We are
not deceived by words or labels, no more than by
the label 'surrealist' than by the label 'communist' or
USSR.'[28] This was a significant issue for Surrealists
who identified with communism, such as S.W.
Hayter. He left the group after they expelled
Paul Éluard and joined the communists, writing to

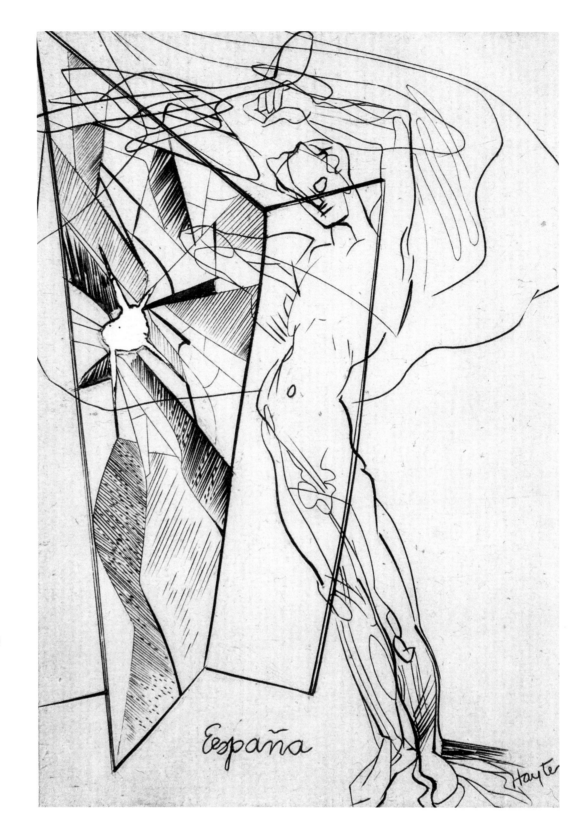

FIG. 104
S.W. HAYTER (1901–88)
España (Fraternity) 1939
Engraving and scorper
on paper
12.7 x 8.9cm
The Sherwin Collection

FIG. 105
S.W. HAYTER (1901–88)
The Runner 1939
Engraving on plaster
26.5 x 20.5
The Sherwin Collection

Trevelyan in November 1938 that he had fallen out with Breton as 'since his interview with Trotsky Breton is anti-Stalin to the exclusion of any other activity ... Their attitude about Spain provoked the last row I had with them. One of the bastards tried to put a crimp in my collection for the Spanish children by suggesting to the person that the money would not go to the kids but to the people who were persecuting their friends the POUM'.[29]

This spirit of 'imaginative freedom' was a quality that characterised the British Surrealists' engagement with the Spanish Civil War. Their refusal to be tied down to the creation of literal, or didactic, works of art reflected their calls for a revolution that had as its object the development of consciousness. After the Nationalist victory in 1939 Penrose painted *The Veteran* (1939, New Orleans Museum of Art, USA) depicting the torso of a Spanish Nationalist general decorated with jewellery, numerous war medals, and a sash in the colours of the Nationalist flag (recalling the official portraits of General Franco by artists such as Ribera Paco), metamorphosed into a macabre petrified tree-stump in a barren and dusty plain. It is a defiant but melancholic work demonstrating how, even in the face of defeat, Surrealist art had the power to subvert nationalism and make a deeper comment on the war.

FIG. 106
JOHN BUCKLAND WRIGHT
(1897–1954)
Fraternité 1939
Copper engraving on paper
12.7 x 8.9cm
The Sherwin Collection

1. Herbert Read, cited in King 1990, p.161.
2. A.L. Lloyd, *Left Review*, 1936.
3. Herbert Read, 'Account of the Conway Hall debate', *International Surrealist Bulletin*, no.4, 1936.
4. Trevelyan 1957, p.72.
5. *International Surrealist Bulletin*, no.4, September 1936.
6. Penrose 1981, p.80.
7. Penrose, *ibid*, p.80.
8. W.H. Auden quoted in Davenport-Hines 1999, p.163.
9. Gascoyne, David, *Journal 1936–7* (London: Enitharmon, 1978), p.43.
10. Spender 1991, p.218
11. Gascoyne, *ibid*, p.45.
12. Roughton, in *Contemporary Poetry and Prose*, September 1936.
13. Roughton, *Contemporary Poetry and Prose*, November 1936.
14. A.L. Lloyd, 'Surrealism and Revolution', *Left Review*, January 1937, p.16
15. Jack Chen in *Artists News Sheet*, January 1938, pp 4–5.
16. James Holland to Roland Penrose, 19 February 1938. SNGMA, Penrose Papers, RPA 0019.
17. Townsend quoted in Forge 1976, p.43.
18. *London Bulletin*, April 1938.
19. The painting was entitled *Abstraction-Anarchist* by Evans when it was first shown at the Whitechapel in 1956. See Gooding 2010.
20. Read 1938.
21. See Freedom 1990.
22. Antony Beevor, *The Battle for Spain 1936–9* (London: Orbis, 1982).
23. Trevelyan, *ibid*, pp 79–80.
24. McWilliam in conversation with Louisa Buck, 1983, quoted in Ferran 2012, p.95.
25. For a number of years Hayter was 'officially' recognised as a Surrealist by André Breton and he took part in the 1936 International Surrealist Exhibition in London. Atelier 17 was named after its address at 17 rue Campagne Première in Paris, where Hayter had moved his workshop in 1932.
26. Letter to Robert Isaacson, 1941, cited in Black 1992, p.49.
27. *Daily Herald*, 2 February 1938.
28. SNGMA Penrose Archives.
29. Hayter to Trevelyan, 6 November 1938. Trinity College Cambridge, Julian Trevelyan papers 16/24.

6 AMONGST THE RUINS: Guernica and its Impact on British Art and Culture

Black as vermin, crawling in echelon
Beneath the cloud-floor the bombers come:
The heavy angels, carrying harm in
Their wombs that ache to be rid of death

C. Day Lewis, from *Bombers*, 1938[1]

FIG. 107.
JOHN ARMSTRONG
(1893–1973)
Windowed Raggedness 1938
Tempera on board
50.8 x 38.1 cm
The Haines Collection

The bombing of civilian targets during the Spanish Civil War marked a fundamental shift in the nature of twentieth-century warfare and in the response of modern artists to such horrors. Much of the Republican propaganda emphasised the human cost of aerial bombing in stark terms by juxtaposing photomontages of individual victims with fleets of planes, as in the iconic posters *Madrid: The 'Military' Practices of the Rebels* (fig. 65 and *HELP SPAIN* (fig. 2). But although the cities of Barcelona, Madrid and Valencia were subjected to intense bombardment by the Nationalist forces during the conflict, it was the annihilation of the ancient Basque capital of Guernica that has come to characterise the suffering of innocent civilians resulting from modern warfare. The town represented the first near-total destruction of an undefended civilian target by aerial bombardment, and as a result the town has become synonymous with Picasso's iconic mural created in response to the atrocity.

The attack on Guernica took place on 26 April 1937, when the centre of the town was busy with civilians for market day. As the nearest military target was a factory on the outskirts of the town (which went unscathed) it became clear that the motivation of the attack was one of intimidating the civilian population and demoralising the Republicans, for whom the Basque region was a stronghold. The Basque government reported at the time that there were 1,645 dead and 889 wounded.[2] It was brought to worldwide attention by the vivid eyewitness account of the journalist George Steer, which was published in both *The Times* and *The New York Times* on 28 April:

At 2 a.m. to-day when I visited the town the whole of it was a horrible sight, flaming from end to end. The reflection of the flames could be seen in the clouds of smoke above the mountains from 10 miles away. Throughout the night houses were falling until the streets became long heaps of red impenetrable debris. Many of the civilians took the long trek from Guernica to Bilbao in antique solid-wheeled farm carts drawn by oxen. Carts piled high with such household possessions as could be saved from

the conflagration clogged the roads all night. Other survivors were evacuated in Government lorries, but many were forced to remain round the burning town lying on mattresses or looking for lost relatives or children, while units of fire brigades and the Basque motorised police under the personal direction of the Minister of the Interior, Señor Monzón, and his wife continued rescue work until dawn. In the form of its execution and the scale of the destruction it wrought, no less than in the selection of its objective, the raid on Guernica is unparalleled in military history. Guernica was not a military objective.[3]

Despite initial claims by the Nationalists that the town had been deliberately burned by fleeing Republican forces, the evidence that the intense aerial bombardment had been carried out by warplanes from Italy and the German Condor Legion, under the command of the Nationalist forces, revealed the Axis Powers' position of neutrality and signing of a Non-Intervention

Pact to be a sham. It gave substance to growing concerns that Guernica had been a testing ground in preparation for a wider European war. For the communist scientist J.B.S. Haldane the bombing of Guernica was 'at the same time an act of terrorism … and a technical exercise for the German air force'.[4] Haldane had witnessed first-hand the bombing of Barcelona during three trips to Spain to advise the Republican government on gas attacks. His subsequent book *Air Raid Precautions*, published in 1938, opened with the warning lines: 'this book is intended for the ordinary citizen, the sort of man or woman who is going to be killed if Britain is raided again from the air'.[5]

Although aerial bombardment of civilians had been used in Abyssinia and China by the Italians and Japanese, as Leo Mellor has asserted, 'it was the Spanish Civil War that had the greatest effect on British culture and fear'.[6] In 1937 the Air Raid Wardens Service was set up in Britain to provide Air Raid Precautions (ARP) advice, report incidents and reassure the public. In the following year the Women's Voluntary Service was established to

FIG. 108
Guernica following the bombardment in April 1937, Black and white photograph International Brigade Archive, Marx Memorial Library

FIG. 109
WALTER NESSLER
(1912–2002)
Premonition 1937
Oil on wood
147 × 199 cm
Courtesy of the Trustees
of the Royal Air Force
Museum, Hendon

support it, with posters designed by the likes of E. McKnight Kauffer, who also contributed posters for Spanish aid (fig. 76). Gas masks were first issued in 1938, and by the outbreak of the Second World War in September 1939 over 44 million had been distributed. In 1940 the connection between the war in Spain and the Second World War was highlighted in a drawing by Olga Lehmann of Spanish refugees in London being fitted with gas masks, that she made after receiving permission from the War Office to make sketches and drawings of air raid shelters and ARP personnel. Three years earlier émigré artist Walter Nessler had expressed this prevalent concern – that the destruction of Spanish cities would prefigure the bombing of Britain – in his painting *Premonition* (fig. 109), in which a gas mask appears on the top of a bombed London skyline. Nessler had kept a scrapbook in which he pasted articles on Spain. In July 1937 he married the sister of the communist artist Felicity Ashbee (who had designed several posters in support of Aid for Spain (figs. 69–71), after having moved from Dresden to London to escape Nazi persecution. In

Premonition London landmarks such as St Paul's Cathedral and the National Gallery appear under a blood red sky amidst the ruins of a bombing raid.

In a less direct way Clive Branson's realist painting *Selling the Daily Worker Outside the Projectile Engineering Works* (fig. 111) suggested the need for an informed working class that would be aware of the political significance of the bombs they were manufacturing. The picture subtly suggests the belief in communist circles that the main victims of a future war to defend capitalism would be the workers themselves. The man and woman selling copies of the *Daily Worker* outside the munitions factory wear aprons bearing the slogan 'For Unity' – a reference to the campaign for unity against fascism. Soon after painting this picture Branson himself was to volunteer to join the British Battalion of the International Brigades to make a direct contribution to the fight against fascism.

In the words of Stephen Spender, writing in 1943, the pre-war art movements such as Surrealism and Abstraction were

FIG. 110
JEAN M. HAMMOND
(DATES UNKNOWN)
Mirroir España December
1937
Gouache on paper
36.6 x 22.1 cm
Ron Heisler Collection

FIG. 111
CLIVE BRANSON (1907–44)
*Selling the Daily Worker
Outside the Projectile
Engineering Works* 1937
Oil on canvas
40.6 x 50.7 cm
Tate: Bequeathed by
Noreen Branson 2004

a reflection in the minds of the more perceptive artists of the volcano of the war which had not yet come to the surface. For years before the war, European cities were unreal, with the unreality of a landscape sunlit and unspeakably silent before a storm. Some artists expressed this violent sense of disorder in surrealism; others by withdrawing into the search for an abstract and integrating symbol. The war is the fulfillment of prophetic visions of art, and in a sense it means a return to reality by artists who found the peace too unreal to be accepted at its face value.[7]

The artist John Armstrong, whose style had associated him with Surrealism earlier in the decade, painted a series of tempera paintings after 1937 featuring the ruins of bomb-damaged buildings. In works such as *Revelations* (fig. 113) and *Sunrise* (fig. 112) the traces of disrupted domesticity – peeling wallpaper, empty hearths on upper floors and broken furniture – are laid open to azure blue Mediterranean skies. These roofless buildings offer

no sense of shelter from the sun, and beyond them are only open, dusty plains. The title of one of the series, *Windowed Raggedness* (fig. 107), alludes to the fate of victims of bombings in Spain and is taken from Shakespeare's play *King Lear*, Act 3, Scene 4:

> Poor naked wretches, whereso'er you are,
> That bide the pelting of this pitiless storm,
> How shall your houseless heads and unfed sides,
> Your looped and windowed
> raggedness, defend you
> From seasons such as these?

In 1936 Armstrong had designed Alexander Korda's surrealist film *Things to Come,* based on H.G. Wells' dream novel, in which 'Everytown' has been destroyed by bombing and remains as a ruin for decades. He had also worked in Rome as a costume designer for the film *I Claudius* in 1937, where he was shocked to observe Mussolini's propaganda and the ubiquitous slogan 'Pro Patria' ('For Country') which accompanied Il Duce's image. The posters peeling from the ruined walls in the painting

Pro Patria (1938, Imperial War Museum) thus presented a comment on the rise of fascism and nationalism in Europe.[8] The filmic image of torn paper blowing down a street (a motif he had admired in the 1927 German movie *Berlin: Symphony of a Great City*) serves to convey a sense of both desolation and fragility. In *The Empty Street* (1938) (fig. 114) the tattered forms suggest, or become metaphors for, human torsos and a dove of peace that is blown into the sky. Despite such symbolism, whilst Armstrong's paintings of ruins were executed in a hyper-real legible style, any 'message' as such was ambiguous and open to interpretation.

There was no mistaking the conviction of Picasso's artistic response to the bombing of Guernica – his iconic mural that formed the centerpiece of the Spanish Pavilion at the 1937 Worlds Fair in Paris (*Exposition Internationale des Arts et Techniques dans la Vie Moderne*). As Myfanwy Evans was to observe in 1937:

Picasso has done an enormous mural for the Spanish pavilion in the Paris exhibition. It is a

FIG. 112
JOHN ARMSTRONG
(1893–1973)
Sunrise 1938
Tempera on board
51 x 76.2 cm
Private Collection

FIG. 113
JOHN ARMSTRONG
(1893–1973)
Revelations 1938
Tempera on board
44.1 x 27.2 cm
Private Collection

FIG. 114
JOHN ARMSTRONG
(1893–1973)
The Empty Street 1938
Tempera on panel
50.8 x 40.6 cm
Private Collection

terrible picture of atrocities that would turn one's hair white if one met them in real life. It is not gently composed to soften the blow, either; not a Laöcoon picture. Nor is it the wild testament of a man distracted by the thought of his tortured country, and least of all is it a 'Red Government' poster screaming horrors to a panic-stricken intelligentsia. It is a passionate recognition of the facts, so purged as to become an almost detached statement, and ultimately so unrealistic as to be almost as abstract as his most abstract painting.[9]

The exhibits in the Spanish Pavilion, designed by Josep Lluis Sert and Luis Lacasa, presented a modernist alternative to the official realist art presented elsewhere in the highly politicised context of the Paris Worlds Fair, which featured the infamous and symbolic stand-off between Vera Mukhina's sculpture of two monumental workers holding a giant hammer at the top of Boris Iofan's Soviet Pavilion and the German Imperial eagle on Albert Speer's Deutsches Haus. Picasso's mural appeared alongside Miró's abstract mural Catalan Peasant in Revolt, Alberto Sánchez Pérez' sculpture The Spanish People Have a Path that Leads to a Star, Julio González' sculpture La Montserrat and Alexander Calder's Mercury Fountain, together with documentary displays featuring a mix of art and propaganda that served to make a point about the value of culture to the Republican government. The Pavilion also featured the films Madrid '36' by Luis Buñuel and Spanish Earth by Joris Ivens and Ernest Hemingway. Picasso had been asked to contribute to the Pavilion by a delegation of Spanish Republicans in January 1937, who were highly conscious of Picasso's status as a celebrated Spanish artist with affiliations to the Left.[10] The previous year he had accepted the post of Director of the Prado, an honorary position that largely served as propaganda for the Republic. As he was to state in May 1937: 'The Spanish struggle is the fight of reaction against the people, against freedom … I clearly express my abhorrence of the military caste which has sunk Spain in an ocean of pain and death.'[11]

Picasso originally considered painting variations on his 'Artist in Studio' theme but did not begin work on the mural until 1 May 1937, just a few days after the news of Guernica had reached the world's media and at which point he found his subject. Over the subsequent five weeks he produced over 67 preparatory sketches and studies as well as the vast cinematic painting. The motifs that feature in both the studies and final work, such as the bull, the horse, a woman with a lamp, a fallen warrior and the mother and dead child, were to go through various permutations and changes as the composition took shape and was recorded in photographs by Dora Maar. Various British artists visited Picasso whilst he was working on the painting, including Duncan Grant, Vanessa Bell and Quentin Bell in May, and Henry Moore and Roland Penrose on 21 June with the Marxist scientist J.D. Bernal. After the Spanish Pavilion opened on 12 July 1937 many more British artists were to visit and see it in the context of the fair, including Merlyn Evans, John Piper and Edward Wadsworth – who considered it 'the only recent nightmarish war painting that I can think of'.[12] The Spanish Pavilion was also to become a stop-off destination for numerous volunteers heading south to fight in the International Brigades in Spain. The Spanish finance minister Juan Negrín believed that, 'in terms of propaganda, the presence of the mural painted by Picasso is equal to a military victory on the front'.[13] However, many in the AIA questioned the appropriateness of Picasso's abstracted formal artistic language for depicting the atrocity and conveying a political message that could be easily understood outside of an informed artistic elite. In his Spectator review of the Paris Worlds Fair art historian Anthony Blunt complained that: 'the gesture is fine, and even useful in that it shows the adherence of a distinguished Spanish intellectual to the cause of his government. But the painting is disillusioning … It is not an act of public mourning, but the expression of a private brainstorm which gives no evidence that Picasso has realised the political significance of "Guernica".'[14]

Later that year Blunt was also to harshly criticise Picasso's pair of engravings The Dream and Lie of Franco (fig. 117), which had been displayed and sold in the Spanish Pavilion to support Spanish Refugee

FIG. 115
Poster for the exhibition of Picasso's Guernica at the New Burlington Galleries, London, October 1938
31.6 × 21.2 cm
The Sherwin Collection

FIG. 116
Installation view of Picasso's Guernica, Weeping Woman, and related drawings on display at the New Burlington Galleries, London, October 1938. Scottish National Gallery of Modern Art, Roland Penrose Papers

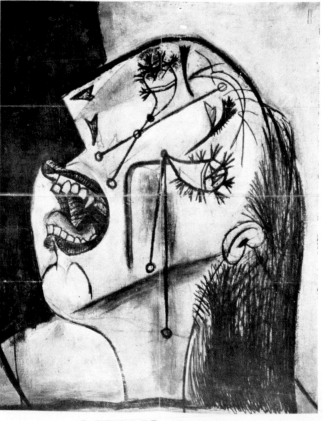

NEW BURLINGTON GALLERIES
BURLINGTON GARDENS — LONDON W.1

VISIT
the
EXHIBITION
of
PICASSO'S

G
U
E
R
N
I
C
A

with over
60
preparatory paintings
sketches and studies
for the composition.

ENTRANCE 1/3

OCTOBER 4TH—29TH
DAILY 10 a.m — 5.30 p.m.

GUERNICA
EXHIBITION

PATRONS

Gerald BARRY, Esq.
Fenner BROCKWAY, Esq.
The Rt. Hon. the Viscount
        CECIL of CHELWOOD, P.C., K.C.
Sir Peter CHALMERS MITCHELL,
        C.B.E., LL.D., F.R.S.
Douglas COOPER, Esq.
Hugh Sykes DAVIES, Esq
Professor Bonamy DOBREE
George EUMORFOPOULOS, Esq., F.S.A.
E. M. FORSTER, Esq.
Victor GOLLANCZ, Esq.º
Ashley HAVINDEN, Esq.
A. P. HERBERT, M.P.
Julian S. HUXLEY, Esq. D.Sc., F.R.S
E. McKNIGHT KAUFFER, Esq.
David LOW, Esq.
D. MITRINOVITCH, Esq.
Mrs. Naomi MITCHESON
P. J. NOEL BAKER, M.P.
The Rt. Hon. Lord NOEL-BUXTON, P.C.
Harry POLLITT, Esq.
Miss Eleanor RATHBONE, M.P.
Ruthven TODD, Esq.
Professor TREND
Peter WATSON, Esq.
Mrs. Virginia WOOLF

ORGANISING COMMITTEE

Chairman: Wilfrid ROBERTS, M.P.
Vice-Chairman: Herbert READ, Esq.
The Rt. Hon. the Earl of LISTOWEL
Hon. Treasurer: Roland A. PENROSE, Esq.
Hon. Organiser: E. L. T. MESENS, Esq.
Hon. Secretary: Mrs. Sybil STEPHENSON

IN AID OF THE NATIONAL
JOINT COMMITTEE FOR SPANISH RELIEF

Relief. Picasso had created them in January 1937 and originally planned for each of the 18 scenes to be reproduced individually as postcards, but the etchings were printed in their present state in an edition of 1,000. Using the format of popular religious prints, known as *alleluias*, Picasso savagely satirised Franco's pretentions to greatness in a comic strip of absurd situations which include caricatures of Franco on a disembowelled horse; dressed in Spanish mantilla; wearing a variety of symbolic hats including the bishop's mitre, cardinal's biretta and the crown; smashing a classical bust; and riding a pig. Several British artists bought copies including Penrose, Henry Moore and Julian Trevelyan. But, in Blunt's view, the engravings could not 'reach more than the limited coterie of aesthetes, who have given their lives so wholly to the cult of art that they have forgotten about everything else.

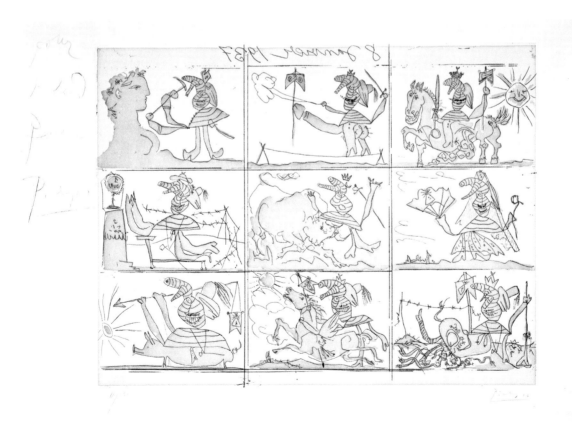

The rest of the world may seem and shudder and pass by. It is not surprising as Picasso's life has been spent in the holy of holies of art'.[15]

Rushing to defend Picasso in a letter to the *Spectator*, Herbert Read pointed out that hundreds of thousands of postcards of Franco cartoons had been sold showing that it was accessible and popular, asserting that:

> it has been said that this painting is obscure – that it cannot appeal to the soldier of the republic, to the man in the street, to the communist in his cell; but actually its elements are clear and openly symbolical. The light of day and night reveals a scene of horror and destruction: the eviscerated horse, the writhing bodies ... It is the modern Calvary, the agony in the bomb-shattered ruins of human tenderness and faith ... It is only too evident to anyone who knows the real facts that the particular form of opposition to modern art adopted by Mr Blunt comes from middle-class doctrinaires who wish to 'use' art for the propagation of their dull ideas.[16]

The lack of legibility was further attacked in the January 1938 *AIA Newssheet*: 'The bad influence of Expressionism, Surrealism, Futurism and Abstraction are too much in evidence. This applies even to the new etchings by Picasso presented to the show, *The Dreams and Lies of General Franco*, that are as fantastic and far less comprehensible than Goya's work in denunciation of war.'[17] Causing the Surrealist Group to threaten to resign from the AIA, this led to an apology in the following month's issue.

The criticism inspired Penrose to seek Picasso's permission to bring *Guernica* to London, so that the 'British public might finally be allowed to judge for themselves whether Blunt's criticisms amounted to more than Marxist dogma'.[18] Writing to Penrose in February 1938 Picasso's friend, the poet Juan Larrea, asserted:

> We want the exhibition to happen with the maximum force and solemnity, both for Picasso himself since the more admired he is the more useful he will be to our cause, and for our cause

itself since thus is one of the rare means we have to reach that sector of the public for whom this kind of argument may prove convincing.[19]

Penrose secured the use of the New Burlington Galleries, which in June 1936 had been the venue for the International Surrealist Exhibition that he had jointly organised with David Gascoyne and Herbert Read. By unfortunate timing, the arrival of *Guernica* in Britain on 30 September 1938 coincided with Prime Minister Neville Chamberlain signing the Munich Agreement with Hitler, Mussolini and Édouard Daladier. The exhibition *Guernica with 67 Preparatory Paintings, Sketches and Studies* ran from 4–29 October, with profits of the sale of the catalogue going towards the National Joint Committee for Spanish Relief. Amongst others, the patrons and supporters included the art historian Douglas Cooper, the Surrealist collectors Edward James and Peter Watson, the authors Virginia Woolf and E.M. Forster, the artists E. McKnight Kauffer, J.C. Stephenson and Humphrey Jennings, and Harry Pollitt of the Communist Party of Great Britain.

In addition to *Guernica* itself and the studies, Penrose included *The Dream and Lie of Franco* and the *Weeping Woman* (fig. 118), the anguished painting he had bought from Picasso in November 1937 together with an etching of the same subject (fig. 119). The motif of the weeping woman had obsessed Picasso whilst he was working on *Guernica* and for months after; he was to make 27 drawings and 9 paintings of the subject. It was based on his lover, photographer Dora Maar, her face grotesquely fragmented to express the tragedy of the war in Spain. Penrose considered it to be 'a postscript to the great mural' that contained a cry of agony caused by the fascist government on humanity',[20] and he commented that the 'eyes themselves, which contain the reflection of airplanes – these engines of destruction which are the cause of her agony – seem to slip from their sockets, capsized like boats in a tempest, while a river of tears runs over the contour of her cheek towards her ear, whose ornamental shape suggests a butterfly sipping the salt of her misery'.[21]

FIG. 117
PABLO PICASSO
(1881–1973)
The Dream and Lie of Franco I and II
8 January and 7 June 1937
Etching and aquatint on paper
38.1 x 57.4 cm
Scottish National Gallery of Modern Art, Edinburgh. Long loan from The Roland Penrose Collection (1997)

FIG. 118
PABLO PICASSO
(1881–1973)
*Weeping Woman
(Femme en pleurs)*
26 October 1937
Oil on canvas 60.8 x 50 cm
Tate, 1987

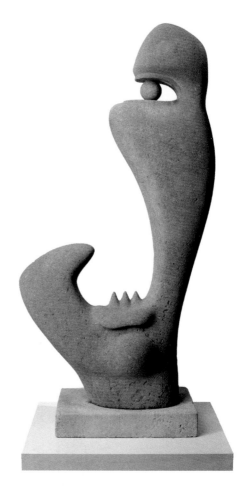

FIG. 119
PABLO PICASSO
(1881–1973)
Weeping Woman
1 July 1937 Drypoint, etching
and aquatint on paper,
dedicated to Roland Penrose
lower right 77.2 x 56.9 cm
Scottish National Gallery of
Modern Art, 1987

FIG. 120
F.E. MCWILLIAM (1909–92)
Spanish Head
1938–9
Hoptonwood Stone
120 x 61 x 23 cm
The Sherwin Collection

The preliminary works (except *Guernica*) were subsequently shown at the end of October in the lecture rooms of Oxford University's Oriel College, sponsored by Oxford Peace Council, where it was described by the reviewer of the *Oxford Times* as a collection of 'horses with maddened expressions, small eyes and ears, and cavernous mouths with bared fangs.'[22] They were also subsequently shown in Leeds Art Gallery in December, together with *Weeping Woman*, before returning to Oxford for another exhibition organised by the New Oxford Art Society and future MP Denis Healey, before being reunited with *Guernica* at the Whitechapel Art Gallery in London in January 1939. The exhibition was opened by Major Clement Attlee, Leader of the Opposition Labour Party and a supporter of the International Brigade, whose Number 1 Company was named the Major Attlee Company in his honour (see fig. 123). Here, in a working-class area of East London, the exhibition attracted over 15,000 visitors in a fortnight (compared to 3,000 at the New Burlington Galleries) – raising over £250 towards Stepney Trades Council's 'Million Penny Fund' to send an East

London food ship to Spain, as well as large quantities of pairs of working men's boots (the price of admission) which were to be sent to the Spanish front. To ensure its message was understood, Eric Newton, Penrose, Read and Trevelyan gave talks to working people about Picasso's work. Trevelyan recalled how he: 'found them ready and eager to accept the various symbolisms ... "That picture's horrible", they repeated at one of the agonised studies for *Guernica*, and indeed Picasso's purpose was just to convey the cosmic horror that he felt at the spectacle of the Spanish War.'[23] The enthusiastic response of the audience was a vindication for Penrose, who commented that 'the misgivings of those who imagined that Picasso's work would mean nothing to the working classes have proved false'.[24]

In February 1939 *Guernica* travelled to Manchester where it was shown in a car showroom in support of the Manchester Food Ship for Spain, before travelling to the US where it was to remain in the care of the Museum of Modern Art until 1981. The tour of Picasso's mural and related studies was to have a powerful and lasting impact on many British artists' work. In the words of Gijs van Hensbergen

FIG. 121
MERLYN EVANS (1910–73)
Distressed Area February 1938
Tempera on canvas over panel
45.5 x 91.5 cm
Collection of Stephen Rich,
London

FIG. 122
HENRY MOORE (1898–1986)
Three Points 1939–40
Cast iron, unique cast
Length: 20 cm
The Henry Moore Foundation:
Gift of Irina Moore

FIG. 123
NORMAN KING
(DATES UNKNOWN)
Clement Atlee speaking in
front of Picasso's *Guernica*
at the Whitechapel Art
Gallery, January 1939
Black and white photograph
22 x 16cm
International Brigade
Archive at the Marx
Memorial Library, London
(Box A-4: S/28)

for British artists it had been a privileged
moment to see the great masterpiece of
twentieth-century art, although many
figures in the art scene, like Blunt, would only
recognise the fact decades later. Only a few
found it inspiring and sustaining in terms of
their own art – its legacy would live on in the
work of John Craxton and Francis Bacon.[25]

The motifs that featured in Picasso's studies were to
be a powerful stimulus for British sculptors seeking
a vocabulary of forms with which to convey the
darkness and violence of their times, such as Henry
Moore and F.E. McWilliam. Moore created the small
bronze *Three Points* (fig. 122) in 1939–40, as Britain
was entering the Second World War. Its piercing
form, as David Sylvester was to note, closely echoes
the screaming mouths and dagger-like tongues that
feature in Picasso's studies for the tormented horse
and wailing mother in *Guernica*.[26] The suggestion
of an anguished scream was also the basis for two
sculptures created by F.E. McWilliam in 1938–9 that
were carved from commercially rejected blocks

of Hoptonwood stone, obtained by McWilliam
during a trip to the Derbyshire quarry with A.H.
Gerrard and Moore. Both *Mandible* (fig. 96) and
Spanish Head (fig. 120) condense the toothy
open mouth of the dying warrior at the base of
Guernica into single three-dimensional forms that
McWilliam described as 'complete fragments'.
Their anthropomorphic qualities serve to express a
palpable sense of horror, with the incompleteness
of the face and interplay of solid and void adding to
the uncanny quality of the work. McWilliam later
recalled that he had seen the Spanish Civil War as
'a case to me of right and wrong. The sculptures
that could be related to that were the *Spanish
Head* which … could be related to *Guernica*'.[27]

F.E. McWilliam's friend Merlyn Evans was also
to reference Picasso's iconic mural, which he had
seen in Paris the previous summer. Evans was a
political radical, but not affiliated to any party. In
a typescript written in early 1938 he stated his
belief that the artist's role in uncertain times was
to present 'the aggressive instinct for power and
destruction' as Picasso had done in *Guernica*.
He also referred to his own painting *Distressed
Area* (fig. 121), painted in London in February
1938, which reflected his outrage at the political
and humanitarian situation in Spain and at British
foreign policy in relation to it. The aggressive
instinct to which Evans referred was embodied
by the angular, menacing forms of the grotesque
androids that occupy the dark landscape, their
saw-toothed and jagged-edged bodies conveying
a palpable sense of threat. In July 1938 Evans
wrote an obscure and nightmarish text in the
style of Wyndham Lewis in which he described an
atmosphere of violence in which the old vulture
'the Carrion King' looks down on a scene in which
'the sky burns like a furnace and in the background
the white-hot embers of a dying cactus arrange
themselves like a dying Roman gladiator wrapped
in the mandibles of a dying crustacean'.[28] Evans
remarked ironically that 'desolation and disaster '
[provide] 'a great age for the satirist'.[29] In the late
1930s and 1940s he painted a series of symbolic
works peopled with semi-abstract figures that
touched upon the political issues of his day,
including *The Massacre of the Innocents* (1937)

which may also have related to events in Spain; *Tragic Group (Victims of Demolition)* (1939–40) which referred to the people displaced by the Russian invasion of Finland; and *Tyrannopolis (The Protestors)* (fig. 124), which although dated 1939 was painted in July 1938, of which he wrote: 'Tyrannopolis is a satire on political economy ... The beginnings of megalopolitan exodus ... cessation of productive work in the arts and sciences.'[30]

The much-debated question of whether Picasso's abstracted artistic style had been a suitable response to the horrors of civilian bombing received an answer of sorts during the Blitz from September 1940 onwards, when 16 British cities were subjected to substantial aerial bombing raids, as had been predicted by J.D.H. Haldane. In the event, John Armstrong found it far less agreeable to paint actual bombed buildings for the War Artists' Advisory

Committee than the imaginary ruins he had painted two years earlier in response to Spain. But others, such as John Piper and Graham Sutherland, drew upon the precedent of Picasso's great mural in their own abstracted depictions of the shattered and twisted bombed buildings. For Sutherland:

Picasso's Guernica drawings seemed to open up a philosophy and to a point a way whereby – by a kind of paraphrase of appearances – things could be made to look more vital and real. The forms I saw in this series pointed to a passionate involvement in the character of the subject, whereby the feeling for it was trapped and made concrete. Like the subject and yet unlike ... Only Picasso however seemed to have the true idea of metamorphosis, whereby things found a new form through feeling.[31]

FIG. 124
MERLYN EVANS (1910–73)
*Tyrannopolis
(The Protestors)*
JULY 1938 - July 1939
Oil on canvas
76 x 91.5 cm
The Sherwin Collection

1. C. Day Lewis, *The Complete Poems by C Day Lewis*, ed. Jill Balcon (London: Sinclair-Stevenson, 1992).
2. Ian Westwell, *Condor Legion: The Wehrmacht's Training Ground* (London: Ian Allan publishing, 2004), p.31. Modern figures suggest that between 153 and 400 civilians died.
3. George Steer, 'The Tragedy of Guernica: Town Destroyed in Air Attack, Bilbao, April 27', *The Times*, 28 April 1937.
4. Haldane, *Precautions* (London: Victor Gollancz Ltd, 1938), pp 47–8.
5. Haldane, *ibid.*
6. Leo Mellor, *Reading the Ruins, Modernism, Bombsites and British Culture* (Cambridge: Cambridge University Press, 2011), pp 22–3.
7. Stephen Spender, *War Pictures by British Artists* (Oxford, Oxford University Press, 1943).
8. This work has frequently been viewed as a specific comment on the Spanish Civil War, and was included in the Imperial War Museum's 2001 exhibition *The Spanish Civil War: Dreams and Nightmares*.
9. Evans 1937.
10. These included José Renau, Director General of Fine Arts, Juan Larrea, the poet and director of information for the Spanish Embassy's Agence Espagne, the architects of the Spanish Pavilion Josep Lluís Sert and Luis Lacasa, the poet Max Aub, and José Bergamin (who had organised the transferral of the Prado's artworks to Valencia).
11. Press statement from May 1937, quoted in Roland Penrose, *Picasso: His Life and Work*, 3rd ed. (London: Granada, 1981), p.315.
12. Wadsworth, quoted in Jonathan Black, *Edward Wadsworth: Form, Feeling and Calculation: The Complete Paintings and Drawings* (London: Philip Wilson, 2005), p.105.
13. Quoted in Fernando Martín, *El pabellón español en la Esposición Universal de Paris en 1937* (Seville: Servicio de Publicaciones de la Universidad, 1982), p.82.
14. Anthony Blunt, *Spectator*, 6 August 1937. Blunt later abandoned his criticism and described *Guernica* in 1957 as 'the last great painting in the European tradition'. See Carter 2001, p.415.
15. Anthony Blunt, *Spectator*, 8 October 1937. According to Blunt's biographer Miranda Carter, after Blunt died in 1983 his executors found one of the limited editions of Picasso's *Dream and Lie of Franco* amongst his possessions, believed to have been bought in 1937.
16. Herbert Read letter, *Spectator*, 15 October 1937.
17. *Artists Newssheet*, January 1938, quoted in Morris 1983, p.43.
18. Hensbergen (2004), p.83
19. Juan Larrea to Roland Penrose, 12 February 1938, Roland Penrose Archive, Scottish National Gallery of Modern Art, RPA 717.
20. Penrose 1981, p.88.
21. Roland Penrose, Roland, *Picasso (Later Years)* (London: The Faber Gallery, 1961).
22. *Oxford Times*, 22 October 1938.
23. Trevelyan 1957, p.88.
24. Penrose in *The London Bulletin*, 8/9 January–February 1939, p.59.
25. Hensbergen 2004, p.96.
26. David Sylvester, *Henry Moore* (London: The Arts Council, 1968), p.36.
27. McWilliam in conversation with Louisa Buck, 1983 in Ferran, *op. cit..*, p.94.
28. Merlyn Evans, quoted in Fraser-Jenkins 1985, p.34.
29. John Armstrong, *Poem and Pamphlet* (1939) quoted in Gooding (2010), p. 54
30. Merlyn Evans, quoted in *Natal Daily News*, 3 April 1940.
31. Sutherland, quoted in Douglas Cooper, *The Work of Graham Sutherland*

HELP THEM TO FORGET

ANNE ACLAND

BASQUE CHILDREN'S COMMITTEE
53 MARSHAM ST. LONDON S.W.I ● ●

7 HELPING THEM TO FORGET: Recording and Supporting Spanish Prisoners and Refugees

FIG. 125
ANNE ACLAND
Help them to Forget:
Poster for the Basque Children's Committee 1937
Off-set lithograph on paper
74 x 52 cm
Courtesy of the People's History Museum

The Spanish Civil War caused a refugee crisis of unprecedented scale, with millions of displaced people in Spain and more than 500,000 in France. Numerous British artists involved themselves in the campaigns to assist these refugees, perhaps most directly through their involvement with the Spanish refugees that came to Britain in the late 1930s. The Basque government made appeals to foreign countries to give temporary asylum to its refugee children, which were given added urgency by the bombing of Guernica in April 1937. Yet, despite widespread outrage in British public opinion at the saturation bombing of the civilian population, the British government still refused to accept the refugees on the basis that it would contravene its policy of non-intervention. A campaign for Britain to accept the Basque children was led by Conservative MP Katherine Stewart-Murray, Duchess of Atholl, in her role as President of the National Joint Committee for Spanish Relief, and Leah Manning, Secretary of the Spanish Medical Aid Committee. The government eventually agreed with great reluctance. However, it refused to take any financial responsibility for the children, demanding that the newly formed Basque Children's Committee guarantee 10/- per week for the care and education of each child. A striking poster designed by the architect Lady Anne Acland was issued by the Basque Children's Committee, featuring a photomontage of a group of refugee children beneath a fleet of bomber planes (fig. 125), calling on the public to 'HELP THEM TO FORGET'.[1]

Almost 4,000 children were evacuated from the port of Santurzi near Bilbao on the steamship *Habaña*, docking at Southampton on 23 May 1937. Although it ordinarily had a capacity of 800 passengers, in fact 3,840 children, 80 teachers, 120 helpers, 15 Catholic priests and 2 doctors were crammed into the ship and even in the lifeboats. Each child was given an identification number marked on a cardboard hexagonal disk pinned to their clothes and printed with the words *'Expedición a Inglaterra'*. They were sent in busloads to a camp on three fields at North Stoneham near Eastleigh in Hampshire, which had been set up by a team of volunteers over the previous fortnight. Over

the subsequent months the 'niños vascos' were dispersed to 'colonies' around the country that were run and financed by volunteers, trade unions, and church groups (the Salvation Army took 400 children, the Catholic church took 1,200). There were several in the south of England including Girton House in Brighton, Aylesbury House in Hove, Penstone House in Lancing, Beach House in Worthing, numerous locations in Southampton, and around 100 across the country from Birmingham and Bradford to Manchester, Newcastle and Swansea, as well as country house estates such as Hurstmonceaux Castle and Lord Faringdon's home at Buscot Park in Oxfordshire. The Stoneham camp was closed in September 1937 following Franco's capture of northern Spain in the summer as the children began to be repatriated, and the majority of children were back in Spain by the outbreak of the Second World War. However, over 400 remained either because they were over 16 and chose to stay or their parents were dead or imprisoned, and around 250 of these stayed permanently.

Whilst her husband Alex Tudor-Hart was serving as a surgeon in the 15th International Brigades in Spain, the communist photographer (and Comintern agent) Edith Tudor-Hart visited the Basque Refugee Camp at North Stoneham in summer 1937. She took a memorable sequence of documentary photographs capturing life in the camp for the children (figs 126–7). Although one image records a group of children with their fists raised in the anti-fascist salute in a gesture of defiance, most of the photographs focus on the children's everyday activities – such as preparing vegetables, playing cricket, and a meeting of English and Basque boys wearing school caps and fedora hats respectively. Born Edith Suschitzky in Austria, Tudor-Hart had studied photography at the Bauhaus School in Dessau, but fled to Britain in 1933 to escape persecution due to her communist activities and Jewish background. A room of the AIA exhibition *Artists Against Fascism and War* in 1935 had been devoted to her photographs of the poverty of working-class life, which sought to engage with their subjects and bring about social change in a way that had much in common with Soviet and German photography of the 1920s. Explaining her views on photography, she stated how it, 'ceased to be an instrument for recording events and became a means for influencing and stimulating events. It became a living art, embracing the people ... In the hands of the person who uses it with feeling and imagination, the camera becomes ... a vital factor in recording and influencing the life of the people and prompting human understanding nationally and internationally.'[2]

The Basque children were also the subject of photographs by another pioneering photographer of the 1930s, Helen Muspratt, a communist and part of the Ramsey and Muspratt partnership that photographed the poet John Cornford. She assisted with organising and fundraising

FIG. 126
EDITH TUDOR-HART
(1908–73)
(Print: Owen Logan)
Basque Refugee Children, North Stoneham Camp, Hampshire 1937
Modern silver gelatine print from archival negative
30.2 x 30 cm
Scottish National Portrait Gallery.
Presented by Wolfgang Suschitzky 2004.
PGP 279.39B

FIG. 127
EDITH TUDOR-HART
(1908–73)
(Print: Owen Logan)
Basque and English School Boys, North Stoneham Camp, Hampshire 1937
Modern silver gelatine print from archival negative
30.1 x 30 cm
Scottish National Portrait Gallery.
Presented by Wolfgang Suschitzky 2004.
PGP 279.36B

FIG. 128
EDITH TUDOR-HART
(1908–73)
*Children arriving
on the Habaña* 23 May 1937
Reproduced in *The Basque
Children in England: An
Account of the Life at
North Stoneham Camp by
Yvonne Cloud* (London:
Victor Gollancz Ltd, 1937).
International Brigade
Archive at the Marx
Memorial Library

for the children to go into homes in England, and recorded many of the children in poignant photographs, as well as the departure of one of the food ships for Spain which left after the scheme was launched in January 1939.

The documentary photographs of refugees within Spain that were taken by the legendary Robert Capa and his contemporaries, and published in magazines such as *Picture Post* (published in England from 1938), were to inspire the work of several painters in Britain, such as Michael Rothenstein – whose *Spanish Refugees* (fig. 129) also gave a nod to the composition of Goya's *The Disasters of War*. But perhaps the most surprising response to such photographs was to emerge from the teenage artist Ursula McCannell. A prodigious talent, at the age of 13 McCannell had been invited by a school friend to spend the Easter holidays of 1936 in the village of Torremolinos in Andalusia. McCannell developed a fascination for Spain and a love of the poetry of Lorca, but also witnessed first-hand the reality of rural poverty and the tensions in society in the months before

the outbreak of the Civil War later that year. Back in England she 'got passionately involved' in the cause and with her father, the painter Otway McCannell who was Principal of Farnham School of Art and a member of the AIA,[3] she closely followed the progress of the war, cutting out articles and reportage photographs from newspapers and *Picture Post*. She and her father even pinned a map on the wall to chart the various battles of the war 'as to where the wicked Francoists had got to'. She began a series of paintings of Spanish refugees fleeing their homes – a desperate and dispossessed mother carrying her children in *Untitled* (fig. 132), or groups of children, the elderly and injured depicted before dramatic glowering skies in *Fleeing Family* (fig. 131). They were executed in a style that owed a debt not only to the expressive figures of El Greco, but also to Picasso's Blue Period, to the work of Stanley Spencer and the gypsy paintings of Augustus John. However, the subject matter was clearly rooted in her collection of press photographs, such as Capa's images of refugees fleeing from Cerro Muriano, 5 September 1936.[4]

FIG. 129
MICHAEL ROTHENSTEIN
(1908–93)
Spanish Refugees 1940
Ink on paper
Current whereabouts unknown

FIG. 130
URSULA MCCANNELL
(b.1923)
Family of Beggars 1939
Oil on board
108 x 79 cm
Marcus Rees Roberts

FIG. 131
URSULA MCCANNELL
(b.1923)
Fleeing Family 1940
Oil on board
86 x 60 cm
The Haines Collection

FIG. 132
URSULA MCCANNELL
(b.1923)
Untitled (Spanish Mother and Children) 1936
Oil on board 61 x 50 cm
Marcus Rees Roberts

Unsurprisingly the combination of Ursula McCannell's skill and the political nature of her work at such a young age drew much attention. She was elected to the Women's International Art Club in 1937, and in 1939 had a solo show at the Redfern Gallery in London, for which reviews in newspapers such as the *Daily Mail* heralded her work 'inspired by war scenes in Spain' declaring that her paintings 'seem to typify all suffering in Spain'.[5] When she exhibited *Waiting* at the United Artists exhibition at the Royal Academy in aid of the Red Cross Fund she was the youngest of 1000 artists exhibited. Her father told the *Evening Standard* in 1939 that, 'just before the Civil War, we were staying in Spain. Revolution was in the air, and Ursula was very much interested by social conditions in Spain. Many of her pictures are based on her memories of old people and children she saw there'.[6] He observed to the *Manchester Evening News* that 'it was after we went to Spain that her work matured and became so serious'.[7]

Clive Branson, serving in the International Brigades, had first-hand experience of the Spanish prisons after he was captured at Calaceite on 31 March 1938. He was incarcerated with many other members of the International Brigades in the Francoist concentration camp in the disused monastery of San Pedro de Cardeña, near Burgos in northern Spain. Accounts of life in the prison by former members of the International Brigades record that the conditions in the camp were overcrowded, insanitary and brutal, and prisoners were subjected to indoctrination and forced to give the fascist salute under threat of shooting. Branson wrote of his experiences of imprisonment, and those of his fellow Brigade-members, in poems such as '*San Pedro*':

> A foreign darkness fills the air to-night.
> The moon betrays this unfamiliar scene.
> Strange creatures, shadow-
> ghosts of what had been
> Live with no aim than groping through half light,
> Talk dreamily, walk wandering, delight
> In trivial acts that formerly would mean
> Nothing. A livid memory, this lean
> Ill-clad rabble of a lost dreaded might.
>
> Look longer, deeper, the accustomed eyes
> Know more than quick appearances can tell.
> These fools, this shoddy crowd, this dirt, are lies
> Their idiot captors wantonly compel.
> These men are giants chained
> down from the skies
> To congregate an old and empty hell.

Later that year Branson was transferred to an Italian-run camp at Palencia, which was the subject of a version of a song that the International Brigades had sung since the Battle of Jarama, to the tune of Red River Valley:

> There's a prison in Spain called Palencia
> 'Tis a place we know all too well
> It was there that we gave of our manhood
> And spent months of misery and hell.
> Surrounded one day by Italians
> Who with guns bought by Chamberlain's gold
> Blown to hell by artillery and avion
> That's how our brave comrades were sold.

FIG. 133
CLIVE BRANSON (1907–44)
*Portrait drawings of members of the British
Battalion of the International Brigade made
in the Prison Camp at Palencia*
August 1938
Pencil on paper
Each 13.6 × 10.8 cm
The International Brigade Archive at the Marx Memorial Library

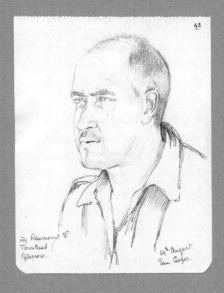

43.

24 Rosemount St.
Townhead
Glasgow.

24th August
Sam Cooper.

37.

3 Castleton Rd
Mitcham
Surrey.

17th August.
Goodwin.

44.

242 Holloway Head
Birmingham.

24th August.
H. Groveck.

34.

Silver Key
8 Michaels Crescent
Primor
Middlesex.

14th August.
Logan.

42.

2 First Avenue
N.W.4 London.

28rd August
Hill.

39.

3 Co-op Cottages
Orford Green.
Warrington
Lancs.

17th August.
Savage.

36.

17th August
Storey.

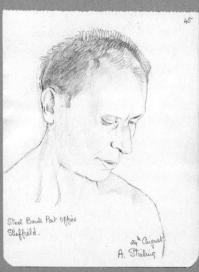

45.

Steel Bank Post Office
Sheffield.

24th August.
A. Stirling

35.

129 Moor End Rd
Lockwood
Huddersfield.

16th August.
Allan Tough.

FIG. 134
CLIVE BRANSON (1907–44)
*Hut Among Trees, Prison Camp
in Spain, Viñalta Spain* 1938
Oil on canvas laid on board
18 x 30 cm
Collection of Rosa Branson

FIG. 135
CLIVE BRANSON (1907–44)
*Landscape from the Prison
Camp, Palencia* 1938
Oil on canvas laid on board
19 x 13 cm
Collection of Rosa Branson

FIG. 136
CLIVE BRANSON (1907–44)
*Inside the Italian Prison Camp
in Spain - Viñalta*
1938
Oil on canvas laid on board
19 x 13cm
Collection of Rosa Branson

FIG. 137
CLIVE BRANSON (1907–44)
Inside the Italian Prison Camp in Spain - Viñalta 1938
Oil on canvas laid on board
20.3 x 28.5 cm
Collection of Rosa Branson

Through family connections (Branson's godfather was Prince Alfonso Bourbon y Orleans infante d'España, who had been at Heidelberg University with Branson's father and a cousin of the former King of Spain) he managed to obtain art materials and painted a series of views of the prison camp on small pieces of canvas – such as *Inside the Italian Concentration Camp, Viñalta, Spain* (1938), *Landscape from the Prison Camp, Palencia* (1938), *Hut Among Trees, Prison Camp in Spain, Viñalta Spain* (1938) and *Inside the Italian Prison Camp in Spain – Viñalta* (figs. 134–7).[8] Rather than emphasise the hardships of the prison, these views of nondescript buildings and trees bleached in strong sunlight are painted in a bold palette that recalls Van Gogh's paintings of fields in the south of France. The poems he wrote at Palencia at the same time, such as *In the Camp,* reiterate his sense of being imprisoned and looking out at the surrounding landscape:

> The storm has cleared the air
> but not barbed wire.
> Here we can bask in the sun,

> Should our eyes have forgotten,
> Pointed at by the guard's bayonet.

> We're like young trees set
> On a wide landscape and mountain
> In a picture for ever certain.
> Clouds pass and fine weather
> and with them the liberty we long for.

In August 1938 at the request of the prison authorities he filled one sketchbook with pencil studies of his fellow British prisoners. These sensitive and accomplished portraits, capturing their individual characters, provide a remarkable artistic record of the International Brigade members. Each is dated and annotated with the name of the soldier and their home address (sometimes pseudonyms and fake addresses were given). Invariably they depict the sitter in profile, reading, or lost in their thoughts. Aware of the constraints on his work Branson wrote a poem titled '*Lines written in a book of drawings done by the order of the Commandant of the Italian Camp*':

These drawings needed a little freedom,
The eye and hand of man enjoying life.
Great Art demands fulfilment of a dream
Of human peace and friendship, no more strife.

In the first years after the Nationalist victory over one million Republican supporters were imprisoned or spent time in labour camps, and approximately 465,000 Republicans fled over the Pyrenees to France in the first winter. They were interned in camps, although approximately 10,000 died before the camps were set up in summer 1939 at Argelès-sur-mer, Saint-Cyprien and Barcarès. After the occupation of France by Nazi Germany during the Second World War 12,000 of the Spanish refugees were sent to Mauthausen concentration camp, but of these only 2,000 survived. The search for both a short-term and long-term solution to the refugee crisis was reflected by posters such as one issued by the National Joint Committee for Spanish Relief calling for food, clothing and money to 'HELP SPAIN'S REFUGEES!' (fig. 139) and to 'Send Spanish Refugee Ships to the new world'. In

April 1939 an appeal was launched to raise £500 to support the cost of rescuing and clothing 35 Spanish artists known to be among the Spaniards interned in concentration camps in southern France, and to send them to Mexico. It was led by the Spanish Artists Refugee Committee, which was a sub-committee of the Artists Refugee Committee that was dealing with Central European refugees fleeing from Nazi persecution. The appeal stated that 'WE AS BRITISH ARTISTS appeal to you to help our Spanish fellows ... show our fellow artists in the camps that we have not forgotten them'. The artist Sir Muirhead Bone, whose book '*Days in Old Spain*' (1936) was based on his extensive travels in Spain in the 1920s, was a prominent supporter. He called on his fellow British artists to support their brothers: 'I am sure that when British artists realise the perilous condition of the Spanish artists in the French camps, they will respond to their urgent need. The ability of these men should be preserved to society. We have a responsibility. The international brotherhood of art is a very real thing. Let us prove it.'[9] In a more direct way, although

FIG. 138
Spanish refugees fleeing over the French border, 1939. Black and white photograph. International Brigade Archive at the Marx Memorial Library (Box 33a: 14)

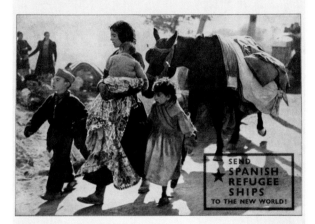

FIG. 139
ANONYMOUS
Help Spain's Refugees! Poster
for the National Joint Com-
mittee for Spanish Relief
c. 1936–9
Off-set lithograph on paper
76 x 50 cm
Courtesy of the People's
History Museum

FIG. 140
HUBERT FINNEY (1905–91)
Spanish Prisoner of War 1938
Watercolour and pencil
on paper
46 x 38 cm
Private collection, Brighton

it was made illegal by the French government, S.W. Hayter gave refuge to Spanish refugees in his Paris studio at Atelier 17 from the spring of 1939. In her diaries author Anaïs Nin recalled how:

> refugees from Spain began to slip into Paris. The laws were rigid: if one sheltered or fed them there would be a punishment of jail and a fine. These were the fighters, the wounded, the sick. Everybody was afraid to help them. William Hayter hid them in his studio …. I was busy cooking gallons of soup, which had to be brought in small containers to Hayter's studio.[10]

Others such as novelist Nancy Mitford (whose sister Jessica had infamously eloped to Spain with Esmond Romilly, communist nephew of Winston Churchill) went to the camps themselves to assist. Mitford joined her husband Peter Rodd in the South of France in May 1939 to work with the relief organisations assisting refugees. The experience inspired an episode of her novel *The Pursuit of Love* in which the character Linda joins

her husband in Perpignan where 'the sight of these thousands of human beings, young and healthy, herded behind wire from their womenfolk, with nothing on earth to do day after dismal day, was a recurring torture'. Mitford confessed that, 'I have never cried so much in all my life'.[11] Although her sister Diana had married leader of the British Union of Fascists Oswald Mosley, and her sister Unity was a fanatical devotee of Hitler, Nancy became resolved in her anti-fascism, writing to her mother, 'If you could have a look as I have, at some of the less agreeable results of fascism in a country I think you would be less anxious for the swastika to become a flag on which the sun never sets ... Personally I would join hands with the devil himself to stop any further extension of the disease'.[12]

The desperate plight of the Spanish prisoners of war caught the imagination of a range of British artists from Henry Moore to the lesser-known Hubert Finney, one of the artists who took part in the AIA's Portraits for Spain scheme.[13] Finney's watercolour portrait *Spanish Prisoner of War* (fig. 140) captures the vulnerability of an older male

whose reddened eyes, forlorn expression and open shirt convey the air of a man broken by his experiences. In contrast, Henry Moore's exploration of the psychological state of imprisonment took a more abstract approach, although still suggestive of the human figure. In drawings such as *Five Figures in a Setting* (fig. 87) Moore had depicted stringed sculptural forms that were contained within an enclosed space suggestive of prison walls. In 1939 he extended this idea in a number of drawings of faces looking out through barbed wire surrounding the internment camps which lead to a drawing and lithograph called *Spanish Prisoner* (fig. 1 and 142). As with his earlier artworks calling for 'Arms for Spain' Moore was conscious of the artist's role in defending democracy. He wrote of how, 'unless he is prepared to see all thought pressed into one reactionary mould, by tyrannical dictatorships – to see the beginning of another set of dark ages – the artist is left with no choice but to help in the fight for the real establishment of Democracy against the menace of Dictatorships'.[14] Although ostensibly abstract, the human power of Moore's *Spanish*

Prisoner comes from the submissive turn of the jaw and the sorrowful eyes that look out from the visor-like frame and barbed wire. Moore had developed the strings that he employed in earlier figures and sculptures to suggest the vertical bars in a prison window, while the atmosphere of apprehension and expression of the human form anticipate his drawings of shelterers in the London Underground during the Blitz. The print was intended to raise money for Spanish refugees held in the detention camps in France, but it was never published due to the outbreak of the Second World War. 'I'm sorry there are no good proofs of the lithograph I started for Spain', Moore wrote to Roland Penrose.

> I only got as far as making 4 or 5 rough trial prints, with the idea of me working on them to get to know what differences to make on each of the stones, when we all got back to London at the end of the summer. The rough prints are stuck up in a row on the wall here at the cottage, and there's plenty I now think I could do, if ever the work on the stones could be

FIG. 141
HENRY MOORE
(1898–1986)
Head 1939
Bronze and string
Reproduced by permission of The Henry Moore Foundation

FIG. 142
HENRY MOORE
(1898–1986)
Spanish Prisoner 1939
Charcoal, wax crayon, chalk, watercolour wash on paper
37.6 x 30.7 cm
The Henry Moore Family Collection

FIG. 143
HENRY MOORE
(1898–1986)
The Helmet 1939–40
Lead
29.1 x 16.5 cm
Scottish National Gallery
of Modern Art GMA 3602

finished. They're at Camberwell School of Art, which is closed – and anyhow as you say, there are no longer any funds to pay the printer, so there's nothing to be done about it at present. But if there's a chance sometime I may go on with it just for my own fun and instruction.[15]

Moore was to realise his ideas for the *Spanish Prisoner* in three-dimensional form in his stringed sculpture *Head* (fig. 141). This lead sculpture, which he was to cast in bronze in an edition of 6+1 in 1968, relates very closely to the drawing and print, even including the suggestion of

eyes which appear in the drawing. Aesthetically *Spanish Prisoner* bridges Moore's abstract works of the mid-1930s and his later humanist work associated with the Second World War. The form was to evolve into Moore's wartime sculpture *The Helmet* (fig. 143), in which a soft figure is encased within a hard metallic surrounding structure suggesting protection and armour. Just as so many artists and intellectuals had predicted, the Spanish Civil War had been the first battle of a major world war, but for many artists such as Moore it had also led to their work as war artists in the conflict that followed.

FIG. 144
Basque Refugees in national costume at the Carshalton Basque Children's Concert (with posters by Anne Acland and Felicity Ashbee) c.1937. International Brigade Archive at the Marx Memorial Library (Box A-3: E/38A)

1. Little is known about Anne Acland (née Alford), except that she was an Associate of R.I.B.A., and married the Liberal MP for Barnstable Sir Richard Acland in 1935. They later gave their estate at Killerton to the National Trust, and he was one of the founders of the Common Wealth Party with J.B. Priestley.

2. Edith Tudor-Hart, notes for an article on 'Photography as a Profession' quoted in R. Radford, 'Edith Tudor-Hart, photographs from the 30s', *Camerawork*, July 1980, pp 1–4.

3. Otway McCannell was one of the participating artists in schemes such as Portraits for Spain in 1938.

4. Within her collection of press photographs are images by Robert Capa of refugees leaving Cerrio Muriano in September 1936, and also his photograph 'On the road from Tarragona to Barcelona, January 15 1939', which shows a refugee cart and horses that has been struck by strafing by fascist planes.

5. F.G. Prince-White, 'Girl Artist is "Seller"', *Daily Mail*, Thursday 11 May, 1939.

6. 'Girl of 16 has Picture in Academy', *Evening Standard*, May 1940.

7. Otway McCannell, *Manchester Evening News*, 11 May 1939.

8. I am grateful to Richard Baxall and Rosa Branson for information on Clive Branson.

9. *35 Spanish Artists: Appeal by the Spanish Artists Refugee Committee*, leaflet, Archive of Henry Sara and Frank Maitland, University of Warwick, Ref: 15C/5/96.

10. Anaïs Nin, *The Diary of Anaïs Nin, Vol III 1939–1944*, ed. Gunther Stuhlmann (New York, Swallow Press, 1969).

11. Charlotte Mosley, *Love from Nancy: The Letters of Nancy Mitford* (London: Hodder & Stoughton, 1993), p.116.

12. Mitford quoted in Laura Thompson, *Life in a Cold Climate – A Portrait of a Contradictory Woman* (London: Headline, 2003), p.140.

13. Finney started his art studies at Bromley School of Art where, in 1918, he won a trade scholarship to Beckenham School of Art. He studied painting under Amy Katherine Browning and etching with Eric Gill. In the mid-1920s he won a scholarship to the Royal College of Art, where he studied under William Rothenstein. In 1929, after graduation, he took up a travelling scholarship, returning to teach part-time at Chelsea School of Art under Percy Hague Jowett and Harold Sandys Williamson, and exhibited with the New English Art Club in the 1930s.

14. Alan Wilkinson (ed.), *Henry Moore: Writings and Conversations* (Aldershot: Ashgate 2002), p.131.

15. SNGMA, Penrose Papers, RPA 0707, 30 October 1939, Moore to Penrose.

SELECT BIBLIOGRAPHY

GENERAL

ADES 1978
Ades, Dawn (ed.), *Dada and Surrealism Reviewed* (London: Arts Council, 1978

BRITT 1995
Britt, David, *Art and Power: Europe Under the Dictators 1930–45* (London: Hayward Gallery, 1995)

BOHM-DUCHEN 2013
Bohm-Duchen, Monica, *Art and the Second World War* (Farnham: Lund Humphries, 2013)

BUCK 1988
Buck, Louisa, *The Surrealist Spirit in Britain* (London: Whitford & Hughes, 1988)

COULTER 2011
Coulter, Riann, *The Surreal in Irish Art* (Banbridge: F.E. McWilliam Gallery and Studio, 2011)

EVANS 1937
Evans, Myfanwy, *The Painters Object* (London: G.Howe, 1937)

GLOVERSMITH 1980
Gloversmith, Frank (ed.), *Class, Culture and Social Change: A New View of the 1930s* (Brighton: The Harvester Press, 1980)

HOWARTH 2009
Howarth, David (ed.), *The Discovery of Spain* (Edinburgh: National Galleries of Scotland, 2009)

MENDELSON 2012
Mendelson, Jordana, *Encounters with the 1930s* (Madrid: Museo Nacional Centro de Arte Reina Sofiá, 2012)

MORRIS 1983
Morris, Lynda and Radford, Robert, *The Story of the Artists International Association 1933–1953* (Oxford: Museum of Modern Art, 1983)

RADFORD 1987
Radford, Robert, *Art for a Purpose: The Artists' International Association, 1933–1953* (Winchester: Winchester School of Art Press, 1987)

READ 1943
Read, Herbert, *The Politics of the Unpolitical* (London: Routledge, 1943)

READ 1940
Read, Herbert, *The Philosophy of Anarchism* (London: Freedom Press, 1940)

REMY 1999
Remy, Michel, *Surrealism in Britain* (Aldershot: Ashgate, 1999)

LEVY 2009
Levy, Silvano and Pirsig-Marshall, Tanja (eds.), *British Surrealism in Context:*

A Collector's Eye (Leeds: The Sherwin Collection, 2009

ZERVOS 1937
Zervos, Christian (ed.), *Catalan Art from the Ninth to the Fifteenth Centuries* (London: William Heinemann, 1937)

ART CATALOGUES, MONOGRAPHS AND BIOGRAPHIES

ALBERT 2011
Albert, Pierre-François and François Albert, *Hayter: Le Peintre – The Paintings* (Montreuil Cedex: Gourcuff Gradenigo, 2011)

AIA 1936
Artists International Association, *Drawings by Felicia Browne* (London: Lawrence & Wishart: 1936)

ARTS COUNCIL 1985
Arts Council, *Edward Burra* (London: Arts Council, 1985)

BEECHEY 2012
Beechey, James and Chris Stephen (eds.), *Picasso and Modern British Art* (London; Tate Publishing, 2012)

BENSON (2008)
Benson, Timothy S, *Low and the Dictators* (London: Political Cartoon Society, 2008)

BLACK 1992
Black, Peter and Désirée Moorhead, *The Prints of Stanley William Hayter* (London: Phaidon Press, 1992)

BRANGWYN 1978
Brangwyn, Rodney, *Brangwyn* (London: William Kimber, 1978)

BUCKLAND WRIGHT 1990
Buckland Wright, Christopher, *The Engravings of John Buckland Wright* (London: Ashgate Editions, 1990)

CARTER 2001
Carter, Miranda, *Anthony Blunt: His Lives* (London: Macmillan, 2001)

DE VERE COLE 2006
De Vere Cole, Diana, *Brangwyn in Perspective* (One Roof Press, 2006)

EDWARDS 1992
Edwards, Paul, *Wyndham Lewis: Art and War* (London: Lund Humphries, 1992)

FERRAN 2012
Ferran, Denise and Valerie Holman, *The Sculpture of F.E. McWilliam* (Farnham: Lund Humphries, 2012)

FORBES 2013
Forbes, Duncan (ed.), *Edith Tudor-Hart: In the Shadow of Tyranny* (Ostfildern: Hanje Cantz Verlag, 2013)

FORGE 1976
Forge, Andrew, *The Townsend Journals: An Artist's Record of his Times 1928–51* (London: Tate Gallery, 1976)

FRASER-JENKINS 1985
Fraser-Jenkins, David, *The Political Paintings of Merlyn Evans 1930–50* (London: Tate Gallery, 1985)

FUNDACIÓN JUAN MARCH 2010
Fundación Juan March, *Wyndham Lewis (1882–1957)* (Madrid: Fundación Juan March, 2010)

GOODING 2010
Gooding, Mel, *Merlyn Evans* (Moffat: Cameron & Hollis, 2010)

GOODING 2002
Gooding, Mel, *Ceri Richards* (Moffat: Cameron & Hollis, 2002)

GORDON 2007
Gordon, Lois, *Nancy Cunard: Heiress, Muse, Political Idealist* (New York: Columbia University Press, 2007)

HOPKINS 1994
Hopkins, Justine, *Michael Ayrton: A Biography* (London: Andrew Deutsch, 1994)

KING 1990
King, James, *The Last Modern: A Life of Herbert Read* (London: Weidenfeld & Nicholson, 1990)

LAMBIRTH 2009
Lambirth, Andrew, *John Armstrong: The Paintings* (London: Philip Wilson, 2009)

LIVINGSTONE 2004
Livingstone, Marco et al, *Kitaj: Retrato de un Hispanista* (Bilbao: Museo de Bellas Artes, 2004)

LOGAN 2011
Logan, Philip, *Humphrey Jennings and British Documentary Film: A Re-assessment* (Farnham: Ashgate, 2011)

MARLER 1993
Marler, Regina, *Selected Letters of Vanessa Bell* (London: Bloomsbury, 1993)

MARTIN 2011
Martin, Simon (ed.), *Edward Burra* (Farnham: Lund Humphries and Pallant House Gallery, 2011)

PENROSE 1981
Penrose, Roland, *Scrapbook 1900–81* (London: Thames and Hudson, 1981)

RAMKALAWON 2013
Ramkalawon, Jennifer, *Kitaj Prints: A Catalogue Raisoneé* (London: British Museum Press, 2013)

SPALDING 1984
Spalding, Frances, *Vanessa Bell* (London: Weidenfeld and Nicolson, 1984)

STEVENSON 2007
Stevenson, Jane, *Edward Burra: Twentieth-Century Eye* (London: Jonathan Cape, 2007)

TOBIN 2013
Tobin, Claudia, *Walter Nessler: Postwar Optimist* (Five Castles Press, 2013)

TREVELYAN 1957
Trevelyan, Julian, *Indigo Days* (London: Macgibbon and Kee, 1957)

SPANISH CIVIL WAR

ARTHUR 2010
Arthur, Max, *Fighters Against Fascism: British Heroes of the Spanish Civil War* (London: Collins, 2010)

BAXALL 2012
Baxall, Richard, *Unlikely Warriors: The British in the Spanish Civil War and the Struggle Against Fascism* (London: Aurum Press, 2012)

BAXALL 2010
Baxall, Richard, Jackson, Angela and Jump, Jim (eds.), *Antifascistas: British and Irish Volunteers in the Spanish Civil War in Words and Pictures* (London: Lawrence & Wishart in association with the International Brigade Memorial Trust, 2010)

BEEVOR 1999
Beevor, Anthony, *The Spanish Civil War* (London: Cassell Military Paperbacks, 1999)

BELL 1996
Bell, Adrian, *Only For Three Months: The Basque Children in Exile* (Norwich: Mousehold Press, 1996)

BOYD HAYCOCK 2012
Boyd Haycock, David, *I am Spain: The Spanish Civil War and the Men and Women who went to fight Fascism* (Brecon: Old Street Publishing, 2012)

BUCHANAN 2007
Buchanan, Tom, *The Impact of the Spanish Civil War on Britain: War, Loss and Memory* (Brighton: Sussex Academic Press, 2007)

COCKBURN 1936
Cockburn, Claud [Frank Pitcairn], *Reporter in Spain* (London: Lawrence & Wishart, 1936)

FREEDOM 1990
Freedom Press, *Spain 1936–1939: Social Revolution and Counter-Revolution – Selections from the anarchist fortnightly Spain & the World* (London; Freedom Press, 1990)

GARCIÁ 2010
Garciá, Hugo, *The Truth About Spain! Mobilizing British Public Opinion 1936–39* (Brighton: Sussex Academic Press, 2010)

GREELEY 2006
Greeley, Robin Adèle, *Surrealism and the Spanish Civil War* (Newhaven and London: Yale University Press, 2006)

HART 1988
Hart, Stephen (ed.), *"¡No Pasarán!" Art, Literature and the Spanish Civil War* (London: Tamesis Books, 1988)

GIJS 2004
Hensbergen, Gijs van, *Guernica: The Biography of a Twentieth-Century Icon* (London: Bloomsbury, 2004)

LOW 1937
Low, Mary and Breá, Juan, *Red Spanish Notebook: The First Six Months of Revolution and the Civil War* (London: Martin Secker & Warburg, 1937)

OTHEN 2008
Othen, Christopher, *Franco's International Brigades: Foreign Volunteers and Fascist Dictators in the Spanish Civil War* (London: Reportage Press, 2008)

PRESTON 2012
Preston, Paul, *The Spanish Holocaust: Inquisition and Extermination in Twentieth-Century Spain* (London: Harper Collins, 2012)

PRESTON 2006
Preston, Paul, *The Spanish Civil War: Reaction, Revolution and Revenge* (London: Harper Perennial, 2006)

PRESTON 2002
Preston, Paul, *The Spanish Civil War: Dream and Nightmares* (London: Imperial War Museum, 2002)

THOMAS 1977
Thomas, Hugh, *The Spanish Civil War* (London: Penguin, 1977)

LITERATURE

AUDEN 1937
Auden, W.H., *Spain* (London: Faber & Faber, 1937)

CUNNINGHAM 1980
Cunningham, Valentine (ed.), *The Penguin Book of Spanish Civil War Verse* (Harmondsworth: Penguin, 1980)

CUNARD 1936
Cunard, Nancy, 'Authors Take Sides on the Spanish War', *Left Review*, 1936

DAVENPORT-HINES 1999
Davenport-Hines, Richard, *Auden* (New York: Vintage Books, 1999)

HEWISON 1977
Hewison, Robert, *Under Siege: Literary Life in London 1939–45* (London: Weidenfeld & Nicholson, 1977)

HYNES 1992
Hynes, Samuel, *The Auden Generation: Literature and Politics in England in the 1930s* (London: Pimlico, 1992)

JUMP 2007
Jump, Jim (ed.), *Poems of War and Peace* (Logroño: Los Libros del Rayo, 2007)

JUMP 2006
Jump, Jim (ed.), *Poems from Spain: British and Irish International Brigaders on the Spanish Civil War* (London: Lawrence & Wishart, 2006)

LEWIS 1952
Lewis, Wyndham, *The Revenge for Love* (London: Methuen & Co. Ltd, 1952)

ORWELL 1938
Orwell, George, *Homage to Catalonia* (London: Martin Secker & Warburg Ltd, 1938)

READ 1938
Read, Herbert, *Poetry and Anarchism* (London: Faber & Faber, 1938)

SKELTON 1964
Skelton, Robin, *Poetry of the 1930s* (Harmondsworth: Penguin Books, 1964)

SLOAN 1938
Sloan, Pat (ed.), *John Cornforth: A Memorial Volume* (London: Jonathan Cape, 1938)

SPENDER 1991
Spender, Stephen, *World Within World* (London: Faber & Faber, 1991)

TIMELINE

1936

20 JANUARY: GREAT BRITAIN
George V dies. Edward VIII
succeeds to the throne.

16 FEBRUARY: SPAIN
In the general elections, parties of the Left
resoundingly defeat those of the Right.
Three days later Manuel Azaña organises
a new cabinet. Among its first acts are
the proclamation of a general amnesty
and the restoration of Catalan autonomy.
Social reform programmes, including land
redistribution, are instigated. Government
opposition to the church resumes.

MARCH: SPAIN
The Falange is banned by the Republican
government. Street clashes take
place between Left and Right.

3 MARCH: GREAT BRITAIN
In response to increasing international
tensions the defence budget rises,
with funds going towards the
Fleet Air Arm for 250 new aircraft
designated for home defence.

7 MARCH: GERMANY
Germany occupies the Rhineland,
denunciating the 1935 Locarno Pacts.

30 MARCH: GREAT BRITAIN
The government publishes its
intention to build 38 warships.

10 MAY: SPAIN
Azaña becomes President of the Republic;
Casares Quiroga becomes Prime Minister.
A wave of strike activity takes place
in cities. Land-hungry peasants seize
landlords' estates in west and south Spain.

30 MAY: ABYSSINIA
Italy formally annexes Abyssinia (Ethiopia)
and incorporates it into Italian East Africa
together with Eritrea and Italian Somaliland.

5 JUNE: FRANCE
First Popular Front ministry under
Socialist party head Léon Blum following
majority in 3 May general elections.
The government institutes a program
of widespread social reform.

12 JUNE – 4 JULY: ART & LITERATURE
International Surrealist Exhibition,
New Burlington Galleries, London.
The British section was selected by
Roland Penrose and Herbert Read.

JULY: ART & LITERATURE
Roland and Valentine Penrose stay at
Mougins with Paul and Nusch Éluard,
Picasso and Dora Maar, Christian and
Yvonne Zervos and Man Ray. Reports of
vandalism and rioting in Catalonia reach
Mougins, and Zervos decides to visit Spain.

4 JULY: ABYSSINIA
Emperor Haile Selassie pleads in vain
for League of Nations assistance in
expelling Italians from his country,
ending the effectiveness of the
League as a force for world peace.

12–13 JULY: SPAIN
Lt José Castillo assassinated by Falangists.
Calvo Sotelo, monarchist leader,
assassinated in reprisal while in Madrid
in custody of state security forces.

17 JULY: SPAIN
The Spanish Civil War begins after Spanish
army units in Morocco proclaim a revolution
against the Madrid government. The
following days the uprising engulfs the
mainland military posts of Cadiz, Seville,
Saragossa and Burgos. But in Madrid and
Barcelona the government resists. The
insurgent leaders, generals Francisco
Franco, Emilio Mola and José Sanjuro, are
supported by all parties of the Right and
clericals, monarchists and conservative
republicans. The rebel leaders have behind
them most of the army and air force, and
huge numbers of North African troops.

20 JULY: SPAIN
Leader of the rebels, General José Sanjuro,
dies near Lisbon as his airplane crashes
on take-off. Of the two remaining
leaders, General Mola is having difficulty
in the north while General Franco is in
full control of Morocco and, even more
importantly, of the veteran Army of Africa.

24 JULY: SPAIN
General Mola establishes a provisional
rebel government, the Junta of National
Defence, in Burgos under General Miguel
Cabanellas. Franco, still abroad, will become
a member of the Junta in early August.

AUGUST: USSR
The Moscow show trials take place at which
senior members of Soviet Communist
Party, Zinoviev, Kamenev and others, are
charged with secretly plotting against Stalin.

6 AUGUST: SPAIN
Franco flies to Seville. At his request Hitler
has supplied transport of aircraft to carry
1500 men of the Army of Africa to Seville,
beginning on 29 July. Italian fighter planes
cover merchant ships carrying 2,500 men
with equipment from Morocco to Spain.

7 AUGUST: USA
The government issues a proclamation of
non-intervention in the Spanish Civil War.

11 AUGUST: ART & LITERATURE
Nancy Cunard arrives in
Barcelona as a journalist.

14 AUGUST: SPAIN
Rebel forces seize Badajoz, carry out
a massacre of the 'reds', and begin
to move eastwards up the Targus
to capture Talavera and Toledo.

19 AUGUST: ART & LITERATURE
An open letter in support of the Republican
government is published in The Times
by signatories including E.M. Forster,
H.G. Wells, Virginia and Leonard Woolf,
J.B.S. Haldane, Julian Huxley, Vaughan
Williams, G.E. Moore and Gilbert Murray.

19–23 AUGUST: USSR
Communist leaders Zioviev, Kamenev
and some of their followers are retried
as Trotskyites, convicted and executed.

23 AUGUST: GREAT BRITAIN
The first British medical unit leaves for
Spain following the formation of the
Spanish Medical Aid Committee to provide
cross-party support to the Republicans.

C.25 AUGUST: ART & LITERATURE
British artist Felicia Browne is killed
on the Aragon front near Tardienta
whilst fighting with a communist
militia she had joined on 3 August.

4 SEPTEMBER: SPAIN
In Madrid a new Popular Front government
is organised under Largo Caballero, in
which both Basques and Catalonians are
represented. Militias are reorganised on
more traditional lines. On the same day,
rebel forces overwhelm Irun, and eight
days later will take San Sebastian.

27 SEPTEMBER: SPAIN
The ancient fortress of the Alcázar in
Toledo, occupied by rebel forces under
Colonel José Moscardó, is relieved after
a two-month siege. Realising the great
propaganda value Franco diverts troops
from Madrid to quell attacking Republicans.

OCTOBER: ART & LITERATURE
Roland Penrose in Catalonia for 7 weeks with David Gascoyne, Christian and Yvonne Zervos and Valentine Penrose. Meets Joan Prats and José Maria Gudiol, visits towns including Vichy, Gerona, Lérida, Tarragona, Barcelona and Valencia. Penrose brings back photos from the front taken by Robert Capa and Gasgoyne in late November with posters for an exhibition at Whitechapel Art Gallery in aid of supplies for Spain.

1 OCTOBER: SPAIN
After a bloodless coup d'etat in Salamanca Franco becomes Spanish Nationalist Head of State in Burgos.

4 OCTOBER: GREAT BRITAIN
'They Shall Not Pass' demonstration in East End of London organised by the Labour Party, the Independent Labour Party and the Communist Party against a gathering of 3,000 fascists.

6 OCTOBER: GREAT BRITAIN
At a party conference Labour rejects the Communist Party for affiliation.

8 OCTOBER: SPAIN
The Basque provinces win from the Popular Front government a promise of home rule. President José Aguirre will lead the first government.

12 OCTOBER: GREAT BRITAIN
Fascist leader Oswald Mosley leads an anti-semitic march through London to Whitechapel.

14 OCTOBER: SPAIN
The first 500 international volunteers to the International Brigades arrive at Albacete, among them poet John Cornford, following a number of British volunteers that have arrived over the past two months.

15–29 OCTOBER: ART & LITERATURE
AIA holds memorial exhibition of drawings by Felicia Browne at 46 Frith Street, London, with a catalogue including a foreword by Duncan Grant. The exhibition raises £260 for the Spanish Medical Aid Committee.

25 OCTOBER: EUROPE
The Berlin–Rome Axis is established between Germany and Italy.

NOVEMBER: ART & LITERATURE
Timoteo Pérez Rubio organises the transferral of 500 artworks from the Prado to Valencia to avoid bombing of Madrid. The British Surrealist Group issue a Declaration on Spain in Contemporary Poetry and Prose.

6 NOVEMBER: SPAIN
Rebel forces begin the siege of Madrid, forcing the government to flee to Valencia. Meanwhile government troops endure heavy rebel air bombardment and widespread street fighting in the suburbs. Defence of Madrid aided by first contingents of the International Brigade.

18 NOVEMBER: SPAIN
Italy and Germany issue proclamations recognising the government of Franco. Britain and France press for non-intervention.

DECEMBER: GREAT BRITAIN
The National Joint Committee for Spanish Relief is set up and chaired by Conservative MP Katherine Stewart-Murray, Duchess of Atholl.

DECEMBER: ART & LITERATURE
Sculptor Jason Gurney travels to Spain to fight in the International Brigades. Artists Help Spain exhibition is organised in London by the AIA. Works donated by Edward Bawden, Vanessa Bell, Jacob Epstein, Eric Gill, Duncan Grant, Augustus John, Lâszló Moholy-Nagy, Paul Nash, Ben Nicholson, Lucien Pissarro, and Eric Ravilious, among others, to raise funds for the field kitchen for the International Column in defence of Madrid.

10 DECEMBER: GREAT BRITAIN
Edward VIII abdicates to marry American-born divorcee Wallis Simpson and is succeeded by his brother as George VI.

17 DECEMBER: SPAIN
Communists expel P.O.U.M. from Catalan Generalitat (government).

1937

JANUARY: ART & LITERATURE
Stephen Spender departs for Spain, joining Wogan Phillips driving an ambulance from Barcelona to Valencia. W.H. Auden drives an ambulance to Spain. Picasso creates the etchings The Dream and Lies of Franco.

2 JANUARY: EUROPE
The Anglo-Italian Mediterranean Agreement is signed, providing for respect of rights and interests in the Mediterranean.

6 JANUARY: USA
Congress passes a resolution that prohibits the shipment of munitions to either side in the Spanish Civil War.

15 JANUARY: ART & LITERATURE
AIA send lorry of medical supplies to British Battalion.

FEBRUARY: SPAIN
The Dean of Chichester, A.S. Duncan-Jones, leads a delegation to the Republican zone and reports that 'there is a strong ant-clerical movement but no anti-God movement in Spain'.

8 FEBRUARY: SPAIN
Franco's rebel forces, reinforced by Italian troops, capture Malaga.

11–12 FEBRUARY: SPAIN
The Battle of Jarama takes place. The British Battalion XV International Brigade suffers from heavy losses; 375 members of the British Battalion are killed on 12 February.

8–23 MARCH: SPAIN
The Battle of Guadalajara sees the Republican Peoples' Army defeat Italian and Nationalist forces attempting to encircle Madrid.

APRIL: ART & LITERATURE
Dean Hewlett Johnson of Canterbury, known as 'the Red Dean', visits the Republican zone. Writer C.F. Forester is invited to visit the Nationalist zone to write articles for British newspapers, but returns shocked by the fanaticism of the insurgents. Conservative MP Katherine Stewart-Murray (Duchess of Atholl), Labour MP Ellen Wilkinson and Independent MP Eleanor Rathbone visit Valencia, Barcelona, and Madrid on a fact-finding mission. This forms the basis of the Duchess of Atholl's book Searchlight on Spain, published in 1938, which sells 30,000 copies.

14 APRIL–5 MAY: ART & LITERATURE
Exhibition for Unity of Artists For Peace, for Democracy, For Cultural Progress in aid of the Spanish Republic is organised by AIA at 41 Grosvenor Square, London, including over 1000 works with separate juries for abstraction, surrealism and others. The First British Artists Congress organised by Nan Youngman, Quentin Bell and Viscount Hastings. The Surrealist Group issues a broadsheet decorated by Henry Moore in support of the AIA International Congress and Exhibition.

17 APRIL: SPAIN
The Popular Front government of Largo Caballero is surplanted by one led by socialist Juan Negrín.

19 APRIL: SPAIN
Franco unifies the Falange and the
Carlists, to secure a sound political base.

26 APRIL: SPAIN
The Basque town of Guernica is
destroyed in a three-hour air-raid by
waves of Nazi German bombers.

MAY: ART & LITERATURE
Wyndham Lewis' novel The
Revenge for Love is published

1 MAY: GREAT BRITAIN
Huge numbers of people take part
in the May Day Parades in London,
including representations from the AIA.

23 MAY: ART & LITERATURE
Paris International Exhibition opens,
with Spanish Republican Pavilion.

23 MAY: GREAT BRITAIN
The steamship Habaña arrives at
Southampton with 4,000 Basque
children – who are accommodated at
North Stoneham in Hampshire, and
subsequently to hostels around England.

28 MAY: GREAT BRITAIN
After the retirement of Stanley
Baldwin Neville Chamberlain
becomes Prime Minister.

JUNE: ART & LITERATURE
Nancy Cunard's 'Artists Take Sides' is
published by Left Review magazine in
3,000 copies, with proceeds going to
Spanish aid. The Chelsea Branch of the
Spanish Medical Aid Committee hold an
exhibition at Whistler's house, including
contributions from Muirhead Bone,
Sir John Lavery, László Moholy-Nagy,
Ben Nicholson and Lucien Pissarro.

16 JUNE: SPAIN
P.O.U.M. outlawed by the Republic.

18 JUNE: SPAIN
Franco's rebel forces capture Bilbao after
protracted combat and numerous air
attacks on the Basque stronghold. Rebels
continue their push toward Santander.

19 JUNE: SPAIN
Bilbao falls to the Nationalists.

24 JUNE: ART & LITERATURE
'Spain and Culture' rally at the Royal
Albert Hall, at which speakers include
Paul Robeson and an auction of
artworks includes a Picasso drawing.

4–18 JULY: ART & LITERATURE
The Second International Congress for
Writers for the Defence of Culture is held
in Valencia. It is attended by Spender,
Sylvia Townsend Warner and Valentine
Ackland, using fake documents as the
British government refused to grant visas.

6–25 JULY: SPAIN
The Battle of Brunete takes place near
Madrid; results in devasting casualties
and a retreat by the Republican Army.

12 JULY: ART & LITERATURE
The Spanish Pavilion opens at the
Paris International Exhibition featuring
Picasso's painting Guernica inspired by
the bombing of the Basque town in April.

18 JULY: ART & LITERATURE
Bloomsbury poet Julian Bell is
wounded at the Battle of Brunete
while serving as an ambulance driver,
and later dies from his injuries.

AUGUST: ART & LITERATURE
Sir Frederick Kenyon, former Director
of the British Museum, and James
Mann, Keeper of the Wallace Collection,
tour the principle art repositories
of the Republican zone and write
positive reports on their return.

5 AUGUST: ART & LITERATURE
George Steer's 'The Fall of Bilbao: An
Eye-Witness's Account' is published
in issue no.6 of Night and Day.

26 AUGUST: SPAIN
Santander, the Republican's last
major stronghold in the North,
falls to the Nationalists.

31 AUGUST: SPAIN
The Republican government moves
from Valencia to Barcelona.

SEPTEMBER: ART & LITERATURE
S.W. Hayter visits Spain at the invitation
of the Republican government.

OCTOBER – DECEMBER:
ART & LITERATURE
John Banting and Nancy Cunard visit
Spain. After Barcelona they go to Valencia,
where they meet American poet Langston
Hughes, and subsequently to Madrid.

NOVEMBER: ART & LITERATURE
Roland Penrose visits Picasso with Paul
Éluard and purchases the Weeping Woman,
which Picasso completed on 26 October.

24 NOVEMBER: ART & LITERATURE
Surrealist Poems and Objects exhibition at
the London Gallery.
Felicity Ashbee designs three posters for
Winter Relief, organised by the National
Joint Committee for Spanish Relief.

28 NOVEMBER: SPAIN
Franco declares a naval blockade
of the Spanish coastline, based on
the island of Majorca – to prevent
resupplying of Loyalist forces.

5 DECEMBER: SPAIN
In the Teruel region the Loyalists
begin a counter-offensive. After
Teruel is captured on 19 December,
momentum of the Loyalists slows.

1938

JANUARY: ART & LITERATURE
Henry Moore, Jacob Epstein and
others attempt to visit Republican
Spain but are denied visas.

15 FEBRUARY: SPAIN
After recapture of Teruel, Franco's
forces begin a dramatic drive
towards the Mediterranean.

MARCH: ART & LITERATURE
The AIA organises a cabaret performance
at the Seymour Hall in London,
featuring work by W.H. Auden and
Benjamin Britten performed by singer
Heidi Anderson and dancers Margot
Fontaine and Robert Helpman.

12 MARCH: AUSTRIA
Austria is declared a province of
the German Reich, completing
the Anschluss (Union).

16–18 MARCH: SPAIN
Heavy bombing of Barcelona
by Nationalists.

16 MARCH: ART & LITERATURE
Realist versus Surrealist public debate
organised by AIA at the Group Theatre
Rooms. Surrealist case argued by Roland
Penrose, Julian Trevelyan and Humphrey
Jennings. Realists represented by Graham
Bell, William Coldstream and Peter Peri.

22 MARCH: GREAT BRITAIN
Demonstration in London in support
of Spanish people organised by the
youth groups of the Liberal Party, the
Labour Party, the Communist Party,
the League of Nations Union, the
Trades Councils and the Universities.

3 APRIL: ART AND LITERATURE
Artist and poet Clive Branson, serving with the International Brigades, is captured at Calaceite and imprisoned.

14 APRIL: SPAIN
Franco's forces capture Vinaroz, thereby splitting the zone held by the Republicans into two.

16 APRIL: EUROPE
Britain and Italy conclude a pact in which Britain promises to recognise Italy's sovereignty in Ethiopia and Italy is to withdraw troops from Spain at the end of the Spanish Civil War.

25 APRIL: ART & LITERATURE
George Orwell's novel *Homage to Catalonia* is published.

1 MAY: ART & LITERATURE
Over 200 artists take part in May Day processions including four Surrealists who dress as Neville Chamberlain.

1 MAY: SPAIN
Negrín offers a 13-point 'peace plan' to the Nationalists, but Franco insists on unconditional surrender.

JULY – SEPTEMBER: ART & LITERATURE
The Victoria and Albert Museum holds an exhibition of etchings and drawings by Francisco de Goya, including *Disasters of War*.

JULY – NOVEMBER: SPAIN
The Battle of the Ebro following Republican attempt to relieve Valencia. Nationalist's counter-offensive is successful, and the Republican army begins to collapse.

JULY: ART & LITERATURE
The Binyon Sisters perform puppet play 'Old Spain' to music by Benjamin Britten at the Mercury Theatre in London

21 SEPTEMBER: SPAIN
Juan Negrín announces the decision to withdraw the International Brigades at the League of Nations, in an attempt to persuade Britain and France to end their arms embargo to the Republic.

29 SEPTEMBER: EUROPE
Chamberlain returns from the Munich Conference having agreed to Nazi demands for the cessation of the Czech Sudeten (German-speaking) lands declaring 'peace for our time'. Picasso's Guernica arrives in Britain.

OCTOBER: ART & LITERATURE
William Coldstream, Claude Rogers, Graham Bell and Victor Pasmore establish the Euston Road School of Drawing and Painting. Clive Branson is released from the camp at Palencia.

4–29 OCTOBER: ART & LITERATURE
Picasso's *Guernica* and studies displayed at New Burlington Galleries, London (3,000 paying visitors) – the drawings tour to Oriel College, Oxford, in late October and Leeds Art Gallery in December.

17 OCTOBER: SPAIN
The International Brigades farewell parade takes place in Barcelona. 305 British volunteers leave Spain.

DECEMBER: ART & LITERATURE
'Portraits for Spain' scheme organised by Ewan Phillips. The exhibition 'From Greco to Goya' is held at the Spanish Art Gallery in London in support of the British Red Cross Society's Spanish Relief fund.

7 DECEMBER: GREAT BRITAIN
The 305 British volunteers who left Spain in October are met at Victoria Station by a crowd of supporters including Clement Atlee, Stafford Cripps and others.

23 DECEMBER: SPAIN
Nationalist invasion of Catalonia begins.

10 DECEMBER – 5 JANUARY 1939: ART & LITERATURE
Ignacio Zuloaga exhibition at New Burlington Galleries in London organised by Nationalist supporters, including a painting in honour of the fascist defenders of the Alcázar of Toledo and El Greco's *Opening of the Fifth Seal*.

1939

JANUARY: ART & LITERATURE
Picasso's *Guernica* shown for two weeks at Whitechapel Art Gallery. Opened by Labour Party Leader Clement Atlee, it has 12,000 visitors.
The anthology *Poems for Spain* is published, edited by Spender and John Lehmann. Hilaire Belloc visits Burgos and meets Franco, subsequently writing articles in *The Tablet*.

26 JANUARY: SPAIN
With Italian assistance Franco's forces capture Barcelona, leading to the end of all Loyalist resistance. Over the next few weeks Franco's forces will capture Catalonia, as 200,000 refugees flee to France.

FEBRUARY: ART & LITERATURE
22 billboard sites made available to the AIA for artists to produce posters appealing for food for Spain.

12 FEBRUARY: ART & LITERATURE
'Arms for Spain' rally in Trafalgar Square features banners based on Goya's *Disasters of War* by Graham Bell – which are then displayed at the AIA exhibition Unity of Artists for Peace, Democracy and Cultural Development at Whitechapel Art Gallery exhibition. 10,000 people attend.

27 FEBRUARY: SPAIN
Great Britain and France unconditionally recognise the Franco government as the sole legitimate regime. This leads Spanish President Azaña to resign.

5 MARCH: SPAIN
Anti-communist coup of Colonel Casado in Madrid, leading to unsuccessful communist revolt.

28 MARCH: SPAIN
Compromise negotiations fail and the Republicans surrender unconditionally, as Madrid and Valencia are handed over to Franco. Franco institutes special tribunals to convict hundreds of Loyalists, despite the protests of France and Britain.

APRIL: ART & LITERATURE
The Spanish Artists Refugee Committee is set up to assist 35 Spanish artists in camps in France. Nancy Mitford works in camps from May 1939. Benjamin Britten's *Ballad for Heroes* is performed at a concert for fallen members of the International Brigades.

11 MAY – 3 JUNE: ART & LITERATURE
Ursula McCannell exhibition in London includes paintings of Spain.

1 SEPTEMBER: POLAND
Without a declaration of war Germany invades Poland. Britain and France issue an ultimatum to Germany.

3 SEPTEMBER: EUROPE
Neville Chamberlain declares that Britain is at war with Germany.

OCTOBER: ART & LITERATURE
Henry Moore produces his *Spanish Prisoner* lithograph, but it is neither editioned nor published due to the outbreak of the Second World War.

LIST OF EXHIBITS

ANNE ACLAND (D. 1992)

Help Them to Forget:
Poster for the Basque Children's Committee
c.1937
Off-set lithograph on paper
74 x 52cm
Courtesy of the People's History Museum

ANON:

What are you doing to prevent this?
November 1936 – May 1937
Half-tone, lithograph on paper
Published by the Ministerio de Propaganda
80 x 56cm
Manuel Moreno

Help Spain 1937
Off-set lithograph on paper
75.5 x 49.2cm
Courtesy of the People's History Museum

Madrid: The Military Practices of the Rebels
1936
Off-set lithograph on paper
Published by Ministerio de Propaganda
66.3 x 49.2cm
Courtesy of the People's History Museum

International Brigade Banner, made and
presented by the Women of Barcelona to
the British Battalion at the farewell parade
of the International Brigades
October 1938
Embroidered banner
160 x 185cm
International Brigade Archive at the Marx
Memorial Library, London

Help Spain's Refugees!
Poster for the National Joint Committee
for Spanish Relief
c. 1936-9
Off-set lithograph on paper
76 x 50cm
Courtesy of the People's History Museum

JOHN ARMSTRONG (1893–1973)

Encounter in the Plain c.1938
Tempera on board
52.1 x 40.6cm
Peter and Renate Nahum

Revelations 1938
Tempera on board
27.2 x 44.1 cm
Private collection

Sunrise, 1938
Tempera on board
51 x 76.2cm
Private collection

The Empty Street 1938
Tempera on panel
50.8 x 40.6cm
Private collection

Windowed Raggedness 1938
Tempera on board
50.8 x 38.1cm
The Haines Collection

FELICITY ASHBEE (1913–2008)

*They Face Famine in Spain:
Send Medical Supplies* 1937
Off-set lithograph on paper
Published by the National Joint Committee
for Spanish Relief
76.3 x 52.1cm
Courtesy of the People's History Museum

*They Face Famine in Spain:
They Needs Clothes* 1937
Off-set lithograph on paper
Published by the National Joint Committee
for Spanish Relief
76.3 x 51.6cm
Courtesy of the People's History Museum

They Face Famine in Spain: Milk 1937
Off-set Lithograph on paper
Published by the National Joint Committee
for Spanish Relief
76.3 x 52cm
Courtesy of the People's History Museum

Study for Milk, in Felicity Ashbee's
Record Book, 1937
Gouache and pencil on paper
23 x 15.4 cm
Estate of Felicity Ashbee

JOHN BANTING (1902–72)

Absolution: Spanish Civil War c.1937-9
Red ink on paper mounted on board
25.4 x 19.1cm
Collection Adrian Dannatt, New York

QUENTIN BELL (1910–96)

May Day Procession with Banner
14 July 1937
Oil on canvas
57 x 41cm
The Faringdon Collection Trust

PEARL BINDER (1904–1990)

Chalking Squad, 1935
Drawing, reproduced in Left Review
Lent by Ruth Boswell

JAMES BOSWELL (1906–1971)

(as 'Buchan')
*What! Not murdered the
Spanish Workers Yet?* 1936
Drawing, reproduced in Left Review
September 1936
13 x 18.5cm
Lent by Ruth Boswell

Speaker's Corner (with Bonner Thompson)
1938
Lithograph on paper
21.6 x 20.3cm
Ron Heisler Collection

FRANK BRANGWYN (1867–1956)

*Poster: For the Relief of Women and
Children in Spain* 1936-7
Lithograph on paper
Published by General Relief Fund for
Distressed Women and Children in Spain
155 x 105cm
Leicestershire County Council Artworks
Collection

Spain c.1936
Lithograph on paper
29.3 x 22.8 cm
Private collection, Brighton

Study for poster '*For the Relief of Women
and Children in Spain*' c.1936
Gouache and chalk on buff paper
28.5cm x 17cm SCAAG 462
On loan from Scarborough Museums Trust

Study for poster '*For the Relief of Women
and Children in Spain*' c.1936
Pencil and gouache on buff paper
25.2cm x 17.4cm SCAAG 463
On loan from Scarborough Museums Trust

Study for poster '*For the Relief of Women
and Children in Spain*' c.1936
Chalk and ink on buff paper
26.4cm x 17.3cm SCAAG 465
On loan from Scarborough Museums Trust

Study for poster '*For the Relief of Women
and Children in Spain*' c.1936
Pencil and gouache on paper
25.3cm x 17.2cm SCAAG 466
On loan from Scarborough Museums Trust

CLIVE BRANSON (1907–44)

Selling the Daily Worker outside
Projectile Engineering Works 1937
Oil on canvas
40.6 x 50.7cm
Tate: Bequeathed by Noreen Branson 2004

Landscape from the Prison Camp,
Palencia 1938
Oil on canvas, laid on board
Signed l.r. CB 1938
19 x 13cm
Collection of Rosa Branson

Inside the Prison Camp in Spain – Viñalta
1938
Oil on canvas, laid on board
Signed Branson 1938
19 x 13cm
Collection of Rosa Branson

Inside the Italian Concentration Camp,
Viñalta, Spain 1938
Oil on canvas, laid on board
20.3 x 28.5cm
Collection of Rosa Branson

Hut Amongst Trees, Prison Camp in Spain,
Viñalta, Spain 1938
Oil on canvas, laid on board
18 x 30cm
Collection of Rosa Branson

Portrait drawings of members of the British
Battalion of the International Brigade made
in the Prison Camp at Palencia
August 1938
Pencil on paper
Each 13.6 × 10.8 cm
The International Brigade Archive
at the Marx Memorial Library

Demonstration in Battersea 1939
Oil on canvas
Signed upper right CB 1939
To Comrade E Marney from EB
40 x 60cm
Collection of Rosa Branson

Daily Worker (July 22) 1939
Oil on canvas laid on board
34.5 x 24.5cm
Collection of Rosa Branson

Noreen and Rosa Jan 1940
Oil on canvas
50.5 x 40cm
Collection of Rosa Branson

FELICIA BROWNE (1904–36)

Self Portrait n.d.
Oil on canvas
33 x 23 cm
Private Collection

Spanish Peasant Woman (standing) 1936
Pencil on paper
28 x 19.7 cm
Private Collection

Spanish Peasant Woman (seated) 1936
Pencil on paper
28 x 19.7 cm
Private Collection

Drawings of Spanish Militiamen and
Women, reproduced in *Drawings by Felicia*
Browne, Lawrence & Wishart, London, 1936
1936
Pencil on paper
Private Collection

Peasant Women 1936
Pencil on paper
15.5 x 11.4 cm
Loaned by Fred Mann in
memory of St. John Mann

JOHN BUCKLAND WRIGHT (1897–1954)

Lenk Asselbergs Kerstmis 1936
Wood engraving on paper
12 x 8cm
Private collection

EDWARD BURRA (1905–1976)

The Watcher c.1937
Watercolour on paper
102 x 67cm
Scottish National Gallery of Modern Art,
Edinburgh.

Medusa 1938
Watercolour, gouache and pencil on paper
155 x 112cm
Manchester Art Gallery

PERE CATALÀ PIC (1889–1971)

Aixafem el Feixisme
(Let's Squash Fascism) 1936
Lithograph on paper
104.6 x 75.5 cm
Manuel Moreno

MERLYN EVANS (1910–73)

Torturing the Anarchist 1937-8
Tempera on canvas
48 x 37cm
Estate of Merlyn Evans

Distressed Area February 1938
Tempera on canvas over panel
45.5 x 91.5cm
Collection of Stephen Rich, London

Tyrannopolis (The Protestors)
July 1938 – July 1939
Oil on canvas
76 x 91.5cm
The Sherwin Collection

HUBERT FINNEY (1905–91)

Spanish Prisoner of War 1938
Watercolour and pencil on paper
46 x 38cm
Private collection, Brighton

SIR TERRY FROST (1915–2003)

Eleven Poems by Federico García Lorca 1989

Lament for Ignacio Sanches Mejias 1989
Etching on paper
55.5 x 37.6 cm
Austin / Desmond Fine Art

Rider's Song 1989
Etching and acrylic paint on paper
55.5 x 37.6 cm
Austin / Desmond Fine Art

It is True 1989
Etching on paper
55.5 x 37.6 cm
Austin / Desmond Fine Art

The Spinster at Mass 1989
Etching on paper
55.5 x 37.6 cm
Austin / Desmond Fine Art

The Moon Rising 1989
Etching on paper
55.5 x 37.6 cm
Austin / Desmond Fine Art

Variations 1989
Etching on paper
55.5 x 37.6 cm
Austin / Desmond Fine Art

Pause of the Clock 1989
Etching on paper
55.5 x 37.6 cm
Austin / Desmond Fine Art

Thamar and Amnon 1989
Etching on paper
55.5 x 37.6 cm
Austin / Desmond Fine Art

San Raphael (Córdoba) 1989
55.5 x 37.6 cm
Austin / Desmond Fine Art

Tree, Tree 1989
Etching on paper
55.5 x 37.6 cm
Austin / Desmond Fine Art

The Old Lizard 1989
Etching on paper
55.5 x 37.6 cm
Austin / Desmond Fine Art

La Luna Asoma (The Moon Rising) 1989
Gouache on paper
Estate of Terry Frost

The Spinster at Mass (Flame Red) 1988
Gouache on paper
Estate of Terry Frost

The Spinster at Mass (Melons and Breasts)
1988
Gouache on paper
Estate of Terry Frost

Duende for Lorca 1987
Screenprint on paper
Estate of Terry Frost

*The Moon Rising (Nobody Eats Oranges
under the Full Moon)* 1976
Gouache on paper
Estate of Terry Frost

FRANCISCO DE GOYA (1746–1828)

Nada el lo dirá (Nothing – The Event will
Tell), from the *Disasters of War*
1810-20, published 1863
Etching, burnished aquatint, lavis,
drypoint and burin on wove paper
Image: 19.6 x 14.5cm
Lent by David Scrase

Madre Infeliz! (Unhappy Mother!)
1810-20, published 1863
Etching, burnished aquatint and drypoint on
wove paper
Image: 17.4 x 12.8cm
Lent by David Scrase

De qué sirve una taza
(What Good is a Single Cup?)
1810-20, published 1863
Etching, burnished aquatint and lavis on
wove paper
Image: 17.9 x 12.6cm
Lent by David Scrase

Enterrar y callar
(Bury them and Keep Quiet)
1810-1814, published 1863
Etching, drypoint, burin, lavis and burnishing
on wove paper; working proof
Image: 16.3 x 23.7cm
Lent by David Scrase

JEAN HAMMOND (1900–1982)

Mirroir Espagna December 1937
Gouache on paper
36.6 x 22.1cm
Ron Heisler Collection

SW HAYTER (1901–1988)

Ayuda a España (Greeting card for 1937-8)
1937
Engraving on Montval paper
Proceeds from sales of this print donated
to the Spanish Children's Fund
Edition of 200
8 x 6.1cm
From the Collection of Alexander,
Patricia and Tresillian Hayter

Paysage Anthropophage
(Man-eating landscape)
17 July 1937
Engaving and soft-ground etching
on paper
Edition of 30
18.4 x 35.1cm
From the Collection of Alexander, Patricia
and Tresillian Hayter

Paysage Anthropophage 1937
Oil on panel
100x 200cm
Private Collection, France

Evacuados 1937
Oil and Gouache on panel
26.5 x 20cm
Private collection, France

Ramblas 1937
Oil and gouache on panel
32 x 19cm
Private collection, France

Casa del Campo 1937
Oil and gouache on panel
37 x 19.5cm
Private collection, France

Runner 1939
Engraving on plaster
Edition of two, in addition to
paper edition of 30
26.5 x 20.5cm
The Sherwin Collection

España (Fraternity) 1939
Engraving and scorper on paper
Edition of 101 for Fraternity Portfolio, in
addition a number of impressions printed
to be pasted onto the Double Crown Club
menu on 11 January 1939 when Hayter
addressed the club on engraving.
12.7 x 8.9cm
The Sherwin Collection

JAMES HOLLAND (1905–96)

*Paris Sketchbook – Comment on Guernica
and Mid-day meeting*, reproduced in
Left Review
July 1937
Lent by Ruth Boswell

NORMAN KING (DATES UNKNOWN)

Clement Atlee speaking in front of Picasso's
Guernica at the Whitechapel Art Gallery,
January 1939, International Brigade
Archive at the Marx Memorial Library

RB KITAJ (1932–2007)

Junta 1962
Oil and collage on canvas
91 x 213 cm
Private collection

La Pasionaria c.1965
Oil on canvas
31 x 33.2cm
Private collection

What is a Comparison? from *Mahler
Becomes Politics, Beisbol* (1964-7) 1964
Colour screenprint and photoscreenprint
on paper
78.5 x 58cm
Pallant House Gallery, Chichester
Wilson Gift through The Art Fund

Go and Get Killed Comrade, We Need a Byron in the Movement, from the series: *Mahler Becomes Politics, Beisbol* (1964-7)
1966
Colour screenprint and photoscreenprint on paper
81.8 x 55.7cm
Pallant House Gallery, Chichester
Wilson Gift through The Art Fund

La Lucha del Pueblo Espanol por la Libertad, from the series: *In Our Time: Covers for a Small Library After the Life for the Most Part* 1969-70
Screenprint on paper
77 x 57.5cm
Pallant House Gallery, Chichester
Wilson Gift through The Art Fund

Kampflieder: Battle Songs: Canzoni di Guerra de las Brigadas Internacionales, from the series: *In Our Time: Covers for a Small Library After the Life for the Most Part* 1969-70
Screenprint on paper
77 x 57.5cm
Wilson Gift through The Art Fund

WYNDHAM LEWIS (1882–1957)

Count Your Dead – They Are Alive 1937
Book jacket
Estate of Mrs G. A. Wyndham Lewis by permission of the Wyndham Lewis Memorial Trust

The Surrender of Barcelona 1934-7
Oil on canvas
83.8 x 59.7cm
Tate, purchased 1947

JAMES LUCAS (DESIGN) AND PHYLLIS LADYMAN (EMBROIDERY)
(DATES UNKNOWN)

British Battalion Banner made by the Artists International Association (replacement for original lost in Spain in 1938)
1938
Embroidered textile
122 x 140cm
The International Brigade Memorial Trust

'LUKE' (DATES UNKNOWN)

Mosley, Collage for *Left Review*
May 1935
Collage on paper
37 x 24 cm
Austin/ Desmond Fine Art

ANDRE MASSON (1896–1987)

La Messe à Pampelone (Mass in Pamplona)
1937
Ink and pencil on paper
80 x 97cm
The Sherwin Collection

URSULA MCCANNELL (B.1923)

Untitled (Spanish Mother and Child) 1936
Oil on board
61 x 50cm
Marcus Rees Roberts

Family of Beggars 1939
Oil on board
108 x 79cm
Marcus Rees Roberts

Fleeing Family 1940
Oil on board
86 x 60cm
The Haines Collection

E MCKNIGHT KAUFFER (1890–1954)

Help Wounded Human Beings: Help to Send Medical Aid to Spain c. 1937
Gouache on paper
57.5 x 42.3
Victoria and Albert Museum

F.E. MC WILLIAM (1909–1992)

The Long Arm 1939
Lime Wood
185cm high
The Sherwin Collection

Mask of Neville Chamberlain for May Day Procession 1938
Painted papier-mâché
19 x 12cm
The Murray Family Collection

Spanish Head 1938-9
Hopton Wood Stone
120 x 61 x 23cm
The Sherwin Collection

COLIN MIDDLETON (1910–1983)

Spain Dream Revisited 1938
Oil on canvas
61 x 51cm
Private collection courtesy of
Karen Reihill Fine Art

The Bride 1938
Oil on canvas
61 x 51cm
Private collection courtesy
Karen Reihill Fine Art

JOAN MIRÓ (1893–1983)

Aidez L'Espagne (Help Spain) 1937
Pochoir with lithographic inscription on paper
31.30 x 24.50 cm
The Sherwin Collection

HENRY MOORE (1898–1986)

Arms for Spain – Cover for *Contemporary Poetry and Prose*, 10, Autumn 1937
1937
Off-set lithograph in bound book
21.5 x 14cm
Private collection, Brighton

Motif for *We Ask Your Attention – Surrealist Declaration* 1938
Printed by the Farleigh Press
The Sherwin Collection

Five Figures in a Setting 1937
Charcoal (rubbed), pastel (washed), crayon on paper
38 x 55.5 cm
The Henry Moore Family Collection

Spanish Prisoner 1939
lithograph in various colours
36.5 x 30.5mm
Uneditioned proofs on English cartridge
The Henry Moore Foundation: gift of the artist 1977

Spanish Prisoner 1939
Charcoal, wax crayon, chalk and watercolour wash on paper
37.6 x 30.7 cm
The Henry Moore Family Collection

Spanish Prisoner 1939
Chalk, watercolour on off-white heavyweight J. WHATMAN wove paper
49.2 x 30.5 mm
The Henry Moore Foundation: gift of the artist 1977

The Helmet 1939-40
Lead
29.1 x 16.5cm
Scottish National Gallery of Modern Art, Edinburgh. Purchased with help from the National Heritage Memorial Fund, The Art Fund (Scottish Fund) and the Henry Moore Foundation 1992

Three Points 1939-40
Cast iron, unique
Length 20cm
The Henry Moore Foundation:
Gift of Irina Moore 1977

ALASTAIR MORTON (1910–1953)

Spanish Civil War 1939
Oil on canvas
68.6 x 91.4cm
Private collection

WALTER NESSLER (1912–2001)

Premonition 1937
Oil on wood
147 x 199cm
Courtesy of the Trustees of the
Royal Air Force Museum, Hendon

ROLAND PENROSE (1900–1984)

Elephant Bird Collage 1938
Collage with paper and string
93 x 70 cm
Victoria and Albert Museum

PABLO PICASSO (1881–1973)

The Dream and Lie of Franco I and II
8 January and 7 June 1937
Etching and aquatint on paper
Each 38.1 x 57.4cm
Dedicated in pencil; 'Pour Roland Penrose,
Picasso'
The Penrose Collection TBC

Weeping Woman 1 July 1937
Drypoint, etching and aquatint on paper
Dedicated to Roland Penrose lower right
77.2 x 56.9cm
Scottish National Gallery of Modern Art,
Edinburgh. Accepted by H.M. Government
in lieu of inheritance Tax on the Estate
of Joanna Drew and allocated by H.M.
Government to the Scottish National
Gallery of Modern Art 2005.

Weeping Woman 26 October 1937
Oil on canvas
60.8 x 50cm
Tate. Accepted by H.M. Government in lieu
of tax with additional payment (Grant-in-
Aid) made with assistance from the National
Heritage Memorial Fund, the Art Fund
and the Friends of the Tate Gallery, 1987

RAMSEY AND MUSPRATT

John Cornford and Ray Peters 1934
Bromide print
30.3 x 36.2cm
Private collection

HENRY RAYNER (1902–57)

There is no Peace 1936
Etching on paper
Signed in pencil
10.7 x 16.5cm
Ron Heisler Collection

There is no Shelter 1936
Signed and titled in pencil
13.2 x 18.3cm
Ron Heisler Collection

FRANCIS ROSE (1921–2006)

*The Reds are Really Not Bad Sorts,
or the Tastes of War* September 1936
Gouache on paper
56 x 44.5cm
Courtesy of Jane England, England & Co.

PRISCILLA THORNYCROFT (B.1917)

All London Friends of Spain Week 1937
Lithograph on paper
75 x 55cm
Private Collection

JULIAN TREVELYAN (1910–88)

Spain 1936
1936 (printed 1972)
Gouache and intaglio print on paper
15.6 x 25.4cm
Courtesy the Bohun Gallery, Henley-on-
Thames

*Horse's Head from the Surrealist Float at the
May Day Procession* 1938
Painted papier-mâché
14.7 x 19.9 cm
Courtesy of the Trevelyan Estate

EDITH TUDOR-HART (1908–73)

*Basque Refugee Children, North Stoneham
Camp, Hampshire* 1937
Modern silver gelatine print
from archival negative
30.2 x 30cm
Scottish National Portrait Gallery,
Edinburgh.

*Preparing Vegetables, North Stoneham
Camp, Hampshire* 1937
Modern silver gelatine print from archival
negative
30.2 x 29.8cm
Scottish National Portrait Gallery,
Edinburgh.

*Basque and English School Boys, North
Stoneham Camp, Hampshire* 1937
Modern silver gelatine print from
archival negative
30.1 x 30cm
Scottish National Portrait Gallery,
Edinburgh.

*Basque Boys Playing Cricket, North
Stoneham Camp, Hampshire* 1937
Modern Modern silver gelatine print
from archival negative
30.2 x 30.1cm
Scottish National Portrait Gallery, Edinburgh

PORTFOLIOS

Solidarité 1938
Portfolio initiated by SW Hayter engravings
by Pablo Picasso, Joan Miró, Yves Tanguy,
André Masson, John Buckland Wright, Dalla
Husband, Stanley William Hayter, with a
poem by Paul Eluard
Engravings on Montval paper, printed by
Henri Hecht
10.2 x 7.5cm
Edition of 150, plus 10 Hors Commerce
Private collection

Fraternité 1939
Portfolio with prints by John Buckland
Wright, Dalla Husband, Josef Hecht, Wassily
Kandinsky, Roderick Mead, Joan Miró, Dolf
Rieser, Luis Vargas and SW Hayter, with
Stephen Spender's poem Fall of a City
accompanied by a French translation by
Louis Aragon.
Etchings on Montval paper, printed by SW
Hayter
Edition of 101, plus Hors Commerce
marked A - L
Approx 12.7 x 8.9cm
Private collection, France

LENDERS, SPONSORS AND SUPPORTERS

PRIVATE COLLECTIONS

Austin / Desmond Fine Art
Rosa Branson
Ruth Boswell
Adrian Dannatt, New York
Jane England, England & Co.
The Estate of Merlyn Evans
The Haines Collection
Alexander, Patricia and Tresillian Hayter
Ron Heisler Collection
Fred Mann, in memory of St John Mann
Manuel Moreno
The Henry Moore Family Collection
The Murray Family Collection
Peter and Renata Nahum
The Penrose Collection
Marcus Rees Roberts
Private collection courtesy of
Karen Reihill Fine Art, Ireland
David Scrase
The Sherwin Collection
The Trevelyan Estate
Estate of Mrs G. A. Wyndham Lewis
by permission of the Wyndham Lewis
Memorial Trust
And other collectors who wish to remain
anonymous

PUBLIC COLLECTIONS

The Trustees of the Faringdon Collection,
Buscot Park
Leicestershire County Council
Manchester City Art Gallery
The International Brigade Archive at
the Marx Memorial Library
The International Brigade Memorial Trust
The Henry Moore Foundation
People's History Museum
Royal Air Force Museum, Hendon
Scarborough Museums Trust
Scottish National Gallery of Modern Art
Scottish National Portrait Gallery
Tate
Victoria and Albert Museum

SPONSORS AND SUPPORTERS
OF THE EXHIBITION

De'Longhi
Elephant Trust
Friends of Pallant House Gallery
Idlewild Trust
International Brigade Memorial Trust
Kirker Holidays
The Mayor Gallery
Henry Moore Foundation
Office for Cultural and Scientific Affairs
Embassy of Spain
Wines from Spain

CONSCIENCE AND CONFLICT
SUPPORTERS CIRCLE

Judy Addison Smith
Vanessa Branson
Keith and Helen Clark
Eden Davies
Lord Garel-Jones and the
Fundación Banco Santander
Goodwood Road Racing Co. Ltd
The Gordon Lennox Family
Elizabeth Hasloch
Angus and Anne Hewat
Denise Holt
John and Caryl Hubbard
Denise Patterson
Simon and Harriet Patterson
Rt Hon Sir Geoffrey and Lady Pattie
Jackie and David Russell
Leslie Silver
Toovey's Antiques and Fine Art
Auctioneers
Warburg Pincus
Willard Conservation
And all those who wish to remain
anonymous

PATRONS OF PALLANT HOUSE GALLERY

We are immensely grateful to the
following Patrons of Pallant House Gallery,
and to all those who wish to remain
anonymous, for their generous support:

Mrs Judy Addison Smith
Keith Allison
Lady Susan Anstruther
John and Annoushka Ayton
David and Elizabeth Benson
Edward and Victoria Bonham Carter
Vanessa Branson
Ronnie and Margaret Brown
Patrick K F Donlea
Frank and Lorna Dunphy
Lewis Golden
Paul and Kay Goswell
Mr and Mrs Scott Greenhalgh
Mr and Mrs Alan Hill
Andrew Jones and Laura Hodgson
James and Clare Kirkman
Peter and Merle Lomas
José and Michael Manser RA
Keith and Deborah Mitchelson
Robin Muir and Paul Lyon-Maris
Angie O'Rourke
Denise Patterson
Simon and Harriet Patterson
Catherine and Franck Petitgas
Charles Rolls and Jans Ondaatje Rolls
Mr and Mrs David Russell
Sophie and David Shalit
Tania Slowe and Paddy Walker
John and Fiona Smythe
Tim and Judith Wise
John Young
André Zlattinger

CURATOR'S ACKNOWLEDGEMENTS

Aspects of the story of the Spanish Civil War have been explored in numerous exhibitions in Spain, Britain and elsewhere, but this is the first exhibition to bring together such a wealth of material relating to British artists and the Spanish Civil War. The exhibition and this book could not have been realised without the assistance of a great many people over the last three years.

First and foremost, Dr Jeffrey Sherwin must be credited for first approaching me with his idea for a show about British Surrealism and the Spanish Civil War. As enthusiastic collectors of British Surrealist art, Jeffrey and his wife Ruth have brought together a very significant group of works relating to Spain, and he has relentlessly sought little-known archive material and ephemera which have helped to enrich the exhibition. We are greatly indebted to all of the private and public lenders to the exhibition, and to the generosity of our Sponsors, Supporters, trusts and foundations and the individual donors who form the Conscience and Conflict Supporters' Circle. Lady Nicholas Gordon Lennox, the Chairman of the Friends of Pallant House Gallery, has worked tirelessly to support this ambitious exhibition. We are also grateful to Anastasia Tennant and Olivia Basterfield and the Arts Council England Government Indemnity Scheme for providing insurance cover for some of the key loans to the exhibition.

I would like to thank many individual people for their valuable help and advice: Pierre-François Albert; Francis Ames-Lewis; David Archer, Austin/ Desmond Fine Art; Annette Armstrong; Catherine Armstrong; Ruth Artmonsky; Christopher Baker, Scottish National Portrait Gallery, Sebastiano Barassi, Henry Moore Foundation; Tracy Bartley; Richard Baxell; Lee Beard; Anne Olivier Bell; Jonathan Black; Ruth Boswell; Ami Bouhassane and Tony Penrose, The Penrose Collection; Steve Bowles; Sophie Bowness; David Brangwyn; Rosa Branson; Victoria Bridgeman; Julius Bryant, peter Ellis, Christopher Marsden, and Martin Roth, Victoria and Albert Museum; Tom Buchanan, University of Oxford; Chris Buckland-Wright; Darren Clark, Charleston; Jonathan Clark; Caroline Collier, Tate; Alex Corcoran and Rosie Micklewright, Lefevre Fine Art; Andrew Cormack, RAF Museum, Hendon; Riann Coulter, F.E. McWilliam Gallery & Studio; Lesley Crewdson; Adrian Dannatt; Andrew Dempsey; Monsieur and Madam Georges Diard; Phil Dunn; Jennifer Dunne and Karen Snowden, Scarborough Museums Trust; Paul Edwards, Graham Lane, Alan Munton, and Nathan Waddell, Wyndham Lewis Memorial Trust; Patrick Elliot and Greta Casacci and Kirstie Meehan, Scottish National Gallery of Modern Art;

Jane England; Carmen Esposito; Eldred Evans; Lord Faringdon and Roger Vlitos, Faringdon Collection Trust; Anita Feldman; Nicholas Finney; Anthony Frost; Adrian Gibbs, Bridgeman; Jonathan Gibbs; Mel Gooding; Jenny Gowing; Sarah Gretton; Dickon Hall; Selena Hastings; Alexander Hayter; Desirée Hayter Levy; Ron Heisler; Gijs van Hensbergen; Wendy Hitchmough; Libby Horner; Simon Hucker, Sotheby's; Patricia Jordan Evans, Bohun Gallery; Jim Jump, Tom Sibley and Marlene Sidaway, International Brigade Memorial Trust; Danny Katz; Carmen Kilner, Basque Children's Association; Ed Kluz; Rose Knox-Peebles; Paul Liss; MJ Long; Anne Lyden; Kate MacGarry; Goshka Macuga; Fred Mann; Conrad and Judy Marshall Purves; Ursula McCannell; Alison McLean; Pandora Melly; Jane Middleton; Mary Moore; Manuel Moreno; Lynda Morris; Alison Morton; Conor Mullen, Redfern Gallery; Andrew Murray; Lucy Myers, Lund Humphries; Chloe Nahum, Carrie Rees and Rosanna Hawkins, Rees and Company; Peter Nahum; Godfrey Omer-Parsons; María de Prada López, Museo Reina Sofia; Robert Radford; Megha Rajguru; Will Rea; Anne and Julian Rea; Benedict Read; Warwick Reeder; Marcus Rees-Roberts; Karen Reihill; Michel Remy; Simon Rendall; Steven Rich; Harriet Richardson, People's History Museum; Robert Robertson; Julian Rothenstein; Jamie Russell-Flint; Enrique Sanz Monge; David Scrase; Harry Smith; Matthew Spender; Stephen Stuart-Smith; Wolfgang Suschitzsky; Jessica Sutcliffe; Bill Thornycroft; Priscilla Thornycroft; Philip Trevelyan; Diana de Vere Cole; Lisa Webb, Leicestershire County Council; David Whiting, Andre Zlattinger and Alice Murray, Christie's and others too numerous to mention.

I am very grateful to Professor Paul Preston who is widely acknowledged as a leading authority on the Spanish Civil War for his insightful foreword to this publication, to Miranda Harrison who has edited the catalogue with efficiency and attention to detail, the catalogue designer David Wynn, Harriet Judd, Head of Commercial and Lucy Myers and the team at Lund Humphries. I would also like to express our gratitude to the Paul Mellon Centre for Studies in British Art for their support of this catalogue, and De'Longhi who are headline sponsors of the Gallery 2014.

At the Laing Art Gallery I would like to thank Julie Milne and Sarah Richardson for enabling the exhibition to tour to Newcastle-upon-Tyne. I would like to thank the trustees of Pallant House Gallery, my Co-Director, Marc Steene and all the staff and volunteers at the Gallery who have assisted with the exhibition, but in particular Assistant Curator, Katy Norris; Curatorial Administrators, Daniella Norton and Sarah Holdaway; the Collections Manager, Sarah Norris; the team of art technicians Andrew Paterson, Louise Bristow, David Miles, Ashley John and Michael Maydon; Elaine Bentley, Head of Development; Andrew Churchill, Deputy Director; Cheryl Gaydon Chilton, Executive Assistant and Anna Zeuner, Head of Communications.

Simon Martin, Artistic Director

PICTURE AND LITERARY CREDITS   INDEX

Pallant House Gallery makes every effort to seek permission of copyright owners for images reproduced in this publication. If however, a work has not been correctly identified or credited and you are the copyright holder, or know of the copyright holder, please contact the Gallery.

© The Estate of Anne Acland: fig.125; John Armstrong, © Artist's Estate / Bridgeman Images: figs. 81, 107, 112, 113, 114; © Estate of Felicity Ashbee: fig.69, 70, 71, 72, 73; ©Anne Olivier Bell: fig.38; ©Estate of Pearl Binder: fig.29; ©The Estate of John Banting / Bridgeman Images: fig.91; © Estate of Winifred Bates: fig. 75; ©Ruth Boswell: figs.28, 30, 83; ©David Brangwyn: figs. 66, 68; ©The Estate of Clive Branson figs. 43, 44, 45, 111, 133, 134, 135, 136, 137; ©The Estate of Felicia Browne: figs.33, 34; ©John Buckland Wright Estate: fig.106; Edward Burra ©Estate of the Artist, c/o Lefevre Fine Art, London: figs. 56, 57, 58, 59, 60; ©Estate of Merlyn Evans: figs. 88, 121, 124; ©Nicholas Finney: fig.140; ©The Estate of Sir Terry Frost: fig.18; ©Estate of Lawrence Gowing: fig.25; © The Estate of Jean Hammond / Bridgeman: fig.110; ©Estate of S.W. Hayter/ DACS, London 2014: figs. 100, 101, 102, 103, 104, 105; ©Bowness, Hepworth Estate: fig.14; ©Estate of Jack Huntington/Viscount Hastings: fig.9; ©R.B. Kitaj Estate: figs. 5,13, 15, 16; © David Low / Solo Syndication: fig.10; ©Courtesy of the artist and Kate MacGarry, London: fig.17; André Masson ©ADAGP, Paris and DACS, London 2014: fig.92; © Simon Rendall: fig.76; © Estate of FE McWilliam: figs. 93, 96, 97,120; ©Ursula McCannell: figs. 130, 131, 132; © Estate of the artist, Colin Middleton /DACS, London 2014: figs. 89, 90; Joan Miró ©Successió Miró/ ADAGP, Paris and DACS London 2014: fig. 98; Reproduced by permission of The Henry Moore Foundation: Frontispiece, figs. 84, 85, 87, 122, 141, 142, 143: © The Estate of Alastair Morton. All rights reserved. DACS 2014: fig.48, ©Estate of Helen Muspratt/ Estate of Lettice Ramsay: fig.37; © Estate of Walter Nessler: fig.109; © The Roland Penrose Estate 2014: Fig. 20; 86; ©Succession Picasso/ DACS, London 2014: figs. 117, 118, 119; © Estate of Pere Catalá Pic: fig.62; ©The Estate of Henry Rayner: fig.11; ©The Estate of Francis Rose: fig.54; © Julian Rothenstein: fig.129; ©Wolfgang Suschitzsky: figs.3, 126, 127, 128; ©Priscilla Thornycroft: fig.79; ©Trevelyan Estate: figs. 95,99; ©The Estate of Mrs G. A. Wyndham Lewis: figs.53, 55.

PHOTOGRAPHY

Christie's Images Limited (2006): fig.48; Faringdon Collection Trust: figs. 25, 38, 51; Gurr John Ltd., London: fig.114; Henry Moore Foundation Archive: figs. Frontispiece, 87, 141, 143, 122, Michael Phipps, The Henry Moore Foundation Archive: fig.142; The Hepworth Estate: fig.14; Tim Higgins Photography: figs. 28, 33, 37 40, 43, 44, 45, 62, 64, 134, 135, 136, 137, 140; International Brigade Archive at the Marx Memorial Library, London: figs.2, 3,6, 8, 12, 35, 39, 40, 42, 46, 52, 63, 75, 108, 123, 138, 144; Courtesy Lund Humphries: figs. 18 and 21; Manchester City Galleries fig.58; Pallant House Gallery, Chichester figs.5, 16; The Penrose Collection: fig.117; People's History Museum: figs. 1, 65, 69, 70, 139; Scottish National Galleries: figs. 57, 116, 119; Trustees of the Royal Air Force Museum: fig.109; Courtesy Royal Albert Hall fig.49; David Chalmers Photography / Scarborough Museums Trust: fig.68; The Sherwin Collection courtesy of Bridgeman Images: figs. 32, 61, 74, 80, 82, 84, 92, 97, 98, 104, 105, 106, 115, 120, 124; Tate, London 2014: figs. 53, 111, 118; Topical Press Agency/ Getty Images: fig.77; Courtesy Diana de Vere Cole: fig.67; Getty Images: fig.77; V&A Images: figs. 76, 86.

LITERARY COPYRIGHT

Excerpt from *Bombers* (1938) , p.111 © Estate of C Day Lewis
Excerpt from *Fall of A City* (1939) , p.69, 105 © The Stephen Spender Trust
Excerpt from *Elegy on Spain* by George Barker , p.73 © Elspeth Barker
Excerpt from *San Pedro* (1938) p.135
In the Camp (1938), p.139, *Lines written in a book of drawings done by the order of the Commandant of the Italian Camp* (1938) p.140 by Clive Branson © Rosa Branson,
Excerpt from *To a Common Priest*, p.97 © Estate of Stanley Richardson